The ABCs of Money

Protecting Your Future Requires
a New Game Plan.

by Natalie Pace

The terms "Stock Report Card," "Stock Report Cards," "Thrive Budget," "3-Ingredient Recipe for Cooking Up Profits," and "The Billionaire Game" are registered trademarks of Natalie Pace.

For Main Street and the 99%

Foreword: Score *and* Defend to Win the Game of Life

by Joe Moglia,
Chairman, TD Ameritrade

I've always said, "No one cares about your money more than you do," but when it comes to debt, it's a different story. Debt collectors care deeply about your money, so deeply in fact that they will call you every single day if you can't pay them. If you don't know how to push back, gain control of the game, and execute a plan that is designed to get everything back on track, you're in trouble. The more time that passes, the more your debt compounds and the more aggressive the bill collectors become.

It's easy to get down on yourself when the debt piles up. Bad choices or bad calls (or bad luck) can make you desperate, particularly if you are trying to save a home you can't afford. Many people make very risky calls when in this situation, hoping that one big bet at Vegas or on Wall Street, or just one more credit card or loan, will win enough money to even the score. High-risk moves like these usually just make the matter worse.

In football, when you are third and long, a "Hail Mary" pass may not be a good call. When it works, it can become almost mythic; the vast majority of the time it falls incomplete or results in a turnover. Here, the successful "Hail Mary" is such a long shot, and the outcome of an incompletion or turnover is so negative, that the best play is sometimes the one that tends to not be all in. When we are talking debt, we could be talking about turning over your house, your car and other valuable possessions and assets to the creditors. This is exactly when you need a great team and an excellent strategy in order to execute your best play with precision. *The ABCs of Money* provides the resources and information you need to assemble your team and game plan.

No matter how difficult things are or how distraught you are, know that others have recovered and gone on to live fulfilling lives. The score right now doesn't have to define who you are or what you are capable of – there is still plenty of the game left to be played. If you are in debt, now is the time to call a time-out, regroup on the sidelines and adjust your strategy.

A sustainable budget and debt reduction strategy are not all "austerity" measures, though, admittedly, it will involve hard choices and sacrifice. Natalie Pace's Thrive Budget emphasizes getting the big ticket spending under control, so that you can have more money for fun, charity and investing – all the things that make life enjoyable and put financial freedom back within reach. That may sound counter-intuitive, but a healthier bottom line and a healthier *you* are necessary to put everything back on track.

As Natalie points out, too many people think they need to pay down debt before they start investing and saving, which is like thinking you can win a football game without any offense. Offense scores; strong defense limits the other team from scoring on you. Compound your gains in a tax-protected retirement account starting with your first job, and you'll have assets that multiply on the scoreboard for the rest of your life. Those points are yours to keep forever, no matter what, so it's very important to start early.

Also, you'll never score a touchdown if you can't run the 100-yard dash. So exercise your money muscles by auto-depositing 10% of your income into your retirement account *first* – before paying any other bill. This is important for three reasons: 1) It increases your assets, which improves your assets to debt ratio; 2) If you aren't doing this, you're just giving your retirement money to Uncle Sam to spend; and 3) In the worst-case scenario, you can borrow against your retirement assets. Once fiscal fitness is a daily habit, you sleep better, enjoy your money more, gain confidence, and find your debt to be a much smaller share of the final score.

The more you are "worth" and the larger your pool of assets, the easier it will be to negotiate better interest rates. High interest rates and penalties can bury you quickly, whereas low interest rates and affordable payments, combined with a sustainable budget and increased assets, can put your life back on track faster. If your debt is completely unmanageable, then you may need to put the "unthinkable" options on the table, and the sooner that you address this head-on, the quicker you can recover.

The ABCs of Money is not just a book for those who are already in trouble. College students need the information before they get their first credit card. Young adults need it before they buy their first home. Empty nesters can use the information to downsize to a sustainable lifestyle, *before* they get into trouble. It's never a good idea to tap home equity to bridge the gap between your expenses and your income, or to buy more home than you can afford, or to make only the minimum payment on a credit card.

Natalie Pace has been in the business of educating, informing and empowering the individual investor for more than a decade. She has made it her life's mission to "transform lives on Main Street." *The ABCs of Money* will teach you how to stop getting buried in debt and start scoring gains for the home team. The more you score, the more you'll win financial freedom and enjoy your life.

Prologue:
2014 Crystal Ball.

As you read *The ABCs of Money*, you'll discover that annual rebalancing is key to maximizing gains because what's hot, what's safe and what's poised to plunge change year to year.

Below are my Crystal Ball Predictions for 2014.

Stocks. Stocks will continue to be on a rollercoaster in 2014, rising and falling, driven largely by politics. There will be many headwinds in the first three months. Congress has to deal with funding the government and raising the Debt Ceiling, on January 15, 2014 and February 7, 2014, respectively. Fitch Ratings has to decide whether or not to downgrade the U.S.' coveted AAA rating (before the end of March). The GDP growth reports through the end of March are predicted to be ugly – perhaps as low as 1% growth. So, in the first part of the year, investing in stocks could leave a sinking feeling in your stomach. By April, however, the economy should get a pickup in GDP growth.

It could pay to get defensive early in the year, lean into stocks at the end of February/March, take some profits in early June, and then ask D.C. in September if they are going to let Wall Street have a Merry Christmas. After a rough start, NASDAQ could end the year up between 8-13%.

Bonds. Bond funds began to lose money in 2013. Smart money is moving out of long-term, riskier bonds and into shorter-term, low-risk opportunities. Make capital preservation your mantra. Don't reach for yield. Keep the terms short and the credit worthiness high. Traditionally, when bonds are vulnerable, the money migrates over to stocks. However, in 2014, the smart money will continue to prefer real estate, solar panels and other hard assets that offer a yield in the form of rental income, savings on your electric bill and potential capital upside. Bonds and bond funds could lose money in 2014, and be increasingly vulnerable in 2015-2016. Credit risk, more than interest rate risk, is the concern.

Gold. Gold took a beating from investors, who were drunk on the returns of stocks, in 2013. Gold mining stocks, in particular, were trading at half of their 52-week high in November of 2013. I'm bullish on gold for the first half of 2014, particularly the gold miners. Gold offers a good hedge against stocks, but, due to the Wall Street rollercoaster, you must be a patient buyer and an opportunistic seller, and have a stomach for risk. When stocks soar, gold sinks, and when stocks stink, gold shines. Buying low and profit-taking early and often offered multiple opportunities for 45%+ gains on gold miners in 2013. Be careful of gold coins, which are often marked up far above the value of gold.

Real Estate. Real estate was on fire in 2013, scoring double-digit gains year over year. Detroit and Las Vegas rewarded investors above 30%. Price increases should slow down in 2014. However, there are still opportunities to buy foreclosures and short sales for those willing to do their research. Income property, if you are strategic about your buying, can still offer one of the best, *safer* returns on investment, with a potential for capital upside, too. (In many markets, the gains are still a bounce off of the low.) Be careful of judicial foreclosure states, many of which are located in the northeastern U.S., because that is an area where prices may be stagnant or have downward pressure. Real estate price gains will be 6-10% in 2014 – more or less depending on your area of the U.S. -- but the potential for income adds to your ROI.

The Best Investment. Solar panels, electric cars and other energy efficiency upgrades to homes and appliances are the best investment in 2014. Every thousand you don't spend on gasoline or electricity is a thousand that stays in your pocket – offering a safe, strong ROI for decades to come. The savings on your gas and electric bills could add up to more than $7,500/year, if you take advantage of every opportunity available to use less gasoline and electricity, and generate more of your own. Tax credits are still available. Solar panel prices are still relatively low-priced.

Hot Industries and Countries. For 2014, clean energy will be back in favor, after a dismal five years. I'm also hot on gold miners and Chile, particularly at early November 2013 buy-in points. Both have the ability to perform well if U.S. stocks wane. The fundamentals of Australia are still good, but the currency and economy cooled off in 2013, so be mindful of your entry and exit points. Utilities are offering strong dividends with relatively low risk, **IF** you make sure their energy generation is not radioactive. Utilities that are mothballing nuclear power plants, and there are quite a few these days, could be vulnerable. Green utilities should withstand Wall Street's storms well, if you buy them at a good price.

If you want ongoing updates on the markets, including my forensic, investigative, financial news, information and education, use the promo code NataliePace to receive a free 90-day subscription to my ezine. Simply go to NataliePace.com and click on Join Now.

Table of Contents

Table of Contents

INTRODUCTION: Stop Making Everyone Else Rich.

I'm going to share something very personal with you. I lost a friend to suicide. This was a number of years ago – before the Great Recession. She was depressed pretty much her entire life, and a bad reaction to her "anti-depressant" drugs surely contributed to the suicide. However, the root of her "dis-ease" was that she made a number of horrible investments. She had pulled money out of a home that she owned free and clear, and lost most of that money by investing on the bad advice of an "accountant friend" who was getting money on the side for putting her in the deal. She also loaned money to a friend who was underwater on a mortgage. The loan was supposed to be temporary – just for 30 days. Her friend ended up declaring bankruptcy, and, though he was paying her back, it was taking years to do it.

She couldn't forgive herself for making these mistakes, and her hatred of those "friends" and experts who advised her was eating her alive. Her desperate circumstance and tragic end fueled my decision to devote my life to educating others on money, and to continue publishing my ezine through thick and thin for over a decade now (where I have saved many homes and nest eggs, in addition to receiving a #1 stock picker ranking).

Today, people are in trouble financially. Over 12 million homes have entered the foreclosure process since the Great Recession, and millions more will be lost before all is said and done. According to Richard Cordray, the Director of the Consumer Financial Protection Bureau, about 30 million U.S. consumers – nearly one out of every ten Americans – is being pursued by a debt collector, for amounts that average $1500 a piece. Far too many are hanging on by a thread to homes they cannot really afford, or have loan mods that are strangling them financially and locking them into an illiquid investment for decades to come.

Others lost too much in their stock portfolio during the Great Recession. Most have recovered at least half of their losses, but fear they are still vulnerable. And you are. If no changes have been made to your portfolio – you are still at risk, big time.

If you got safe in bonds during the Great Recession (good move), you are not as safe as you think – even with the borrowed promise from the central banks that they'll keep interest rates low for years to come. Rock bottom interest rates at the European Central Bank didn't stop Greece from having to offer 20%+ interest rates to attract borrowers. It's no secret that the U.S. government, states and cities are carrying high debt. Did you know that many of your favorite Blue Chip corporations are, too?

Once you get into financial trouble, the banks and credit card companies keep you backed into a corner, so that paying them is at the top of your mind, even before taking care of your own financial future. While you are fretting about being honorable, getting your life back on track, making payments on time and "keeping your FICO score up," taking the matter quite personally, the debt collector on the other end of the line is trained to take emotions out of it and stick to the business of getting paid. That's their job. It's not their job to inform you of all of your rights and responsibilities (which they probably don't even know), or to offer solutions to put you on the path to financial freedom and get your financial house cleaned up once and for all. It's their job to try and get as much money out of you as they can, for as long as they can and to make sure that they are first in line whenever any income arrives. And because time is limited and you assume that they want to work with you honorably, you might be relying on your adversary for advice. And yes, the debt collector, once it gets to that point, is your adversary.

Meanwhile, you lose sleep. You get upset every time they call and hound you for money that you simply don't have. Your health might suffer. You might be short with those you love, take on extra debt or make a big gamble to try and win a jackpot. In fact, it is in these desperate moments that you are most susceptible to the scam artist, hoping for that big win and willing to try or believe almost anything to get it.

It is sad to acknowledge, but a lot of folks get suicidal or homicidal in this situation. During the Great Recession, there were far too many people who were underwater on their home mortgage, who, after failing to get a loan modification, thought the only way out was to take their own life. None of these things remedy the situation; all of them make matters worse. And the legal options, which could save your home and give you a second shot, are never even considered. The lifeboat and lifelines that are available to you sit idle, or worse, are sunk in a desperate, ill-advised attempt to right the situation.

Yes. Even in the worst-case scenario, there are many options. There are many possibilities on the menu of debt reduction that are simply not well publicized. And they have ugly sounding names that keep a lot of people from ever considering them. There are extraordinary possibilities for investments – safe, hard assets with a great return – that most people don't think they can qualify for, or are just so beaten up by making bad investments that they have no faith in anything, except the Apocalypse and the gold ads that promise to be the only thing worthwhile when the entire financial system melts down.

When you are underwater on a mortgage or behind on your credit card payments, you can expect aggressive calls from some pretty relentless debt collectors, who walk as close to the line of what is legal as they possibly can. They will use every psychological strategy known to man – including making you feel like their friend, or conversely, insulting you or threatening to put a lien on your income and assets – to make sure that paying them back is paramount in your mind, even above making sure you've got your own assets covered (which should always be your *first* financial job). They'll threaten you with liens, late fees, high interest rates, low FICO scores and make you feel like missed payments are worse than felony manslaughter.

Once you realize that you are the author of your life and you are the only one responsible for taking care of you and your family, you can stop letting the daily threats of the debt collector define your financial strategy. Following the tenets of *The ABCs of Money* will lead you out of today's crisis and into tomorrow's much more prosperous and fulfilling life and lifestyle.

Part 1: Debt

Chapter 1: How Can I Pay Off My Credits Cards?

A 10-Step Plan for Getting Out of Debt Forever.

In 2011, the number one question searched for was, "How can I pay off my credit card?" (according to AOL). That is not surprising since at least 30 million Americans are being hounded by debt collectors. According to the Federal Reserve Bank of New York, $672 billion was owed on credit cards and $914 billion on student loans, as of July 2012. That averages to over $5,000 per person.

What a lot of people don't realize is that even if you make timely and regular payments on your credit card debt, your credit score and debt load could be getting worse. New credit and types of credit in use account for 20% of your score. Your "amount owed" (debt to assets ratio) is a whopping 30% of the score. That is increasing if you are making minimum payments and/or if the value of what you purchased is declining. And if you are making payments, but not using your credit cards because they are maxed out, that is reducing your score as well.

Fear of FICO score has frozen a lot of people into staying with a bad idea, a bad investment and often even an unsustainable lifestyle. Are you stuck in an underwater mortgage on a home that is just too expensive for you? Are you stuck in a city, when your career would do better elsewhere? (We'll talk about how to fix that in the Real Estate section of this book.)

In troubled economic times, the longer you wait to fix things, the worse things get.

Credit Scoring:

PAYMENT HISTORY 35% – Are payments late? If so, how late? How often? Which accounts?

AMOUNTS OWED 30% – What are your account balances? Are your accounts "maxed out"? Are you underwater? Did the home, car or investment you financed lose money?

LENGTH OF CREDIT 15% – How long has each account been open? When was it last used?

TYPES OF CREDIT IN USE 10% – Do you have a good mix of credit? How many accounts do you have open?

NEW CREDIT 10% – How many new accounts do you have? How long since you opened an account? Are you in good standing? How long have you been in good standing?

In most, but not all, cases, making payments on your debt is a *piece* of the solution, but it is never the entire strategy. You have to address the lifestyle and money habits that got you in trouble in the first place. In the case of a home or car, or other big-ticket item that is declining in value, which you can't afford, you need an exit strategy. Credit Card Counseling and Debt Managers may help – or they may hurt, depending on how long they have been around and what their motivations are for being in business in the first place. Debt restructuring, through the bankruptcy courts, is not the best option for everyone, but it is an option that anyone who is severely indebted, with little hope of paying the debt off, should put on the table early in the game. The sooner you restructure your debt and lifestyle, the sooner that you can start rebuilding your life and credit score.

Never, ever, borrow from IRA to pay "Paul." Withdrawing money from your IRA (or 401k, annuity, or any retirement plan) to pay down your credit cards or mortgage is a bad idea for many, many reasons, including the most important one – that money is yours to keep, no matter what. With all of the taxes and penalties of an early withdrawal, you could be losing half of the money you are trying to tap.

No one can take you to court and drain your retirement accounts – not even in the case of murder. (Just ask OJ Simpson.) If you are thinking of draining your nest egg, then your lifestyle is too expensive. It is your budget, not your nest egg, that needs to be revamped. (I repeat: never give your retirement money to a debt collector. That is your lifeboat.)

Only borrow from other sources, such as home equity, if it is a part of a well-developed strategy that includes expense reduction, a new budget and a plan that will position you better going forward. Why? If you don't change the habits that got you into debt in the first place, borrowing more money is only a temporary fix that will dig the hole deeper going forward.

So, now that you have a few basic rules, let's learn the 10 steps that will eliminate the debt and make sure you are never in this position again...

A 10-Step Plan for Getting Out of Debt Forever.

1. **Pay Yourself First.**
2. **Increase Income.**
3. **Decrease Expenses.**
4. **The Big Three: Housing, Transportation & Insurance.**
5. **Health Savings Accounts.**
6. **Debt Consolidation.**
7. **Credit Counseling.**
8. **Personal Bankruptcy.**

9. **The Thrive Budget.**

10. **Financial Education.**

And here are the details…

1. **Pay Yourself First.** You will never *earn* your way to
   financial freedom. If you don't invest your money well,
   then the minute you lose your job or retire, your lifestyle
   will go downhill fast. Financial freedom is a result of
   investing well, not just "doing a good job." Put 10% of
   your income into a tax protected retirement account as
   the first thing you do *even when you are in debt.*

   Why? Debt collectors use the power of
   compounding to their benefit; you can use it to yours. If
   you save 10% and that 10% earns 10% (what stocks and
   bonds have done for the past 30 years), then you will
   have more money than you earn in seven short years
   and your money will make more than you do within 25
   years. Teens who start investing wisely with their first
   job could retire before they are 50.

   Retirement plans in the U.S. are protected from all
   financial predators, even debt collectors and even in the
   worst-case scenario of bankruptcy or foreclosure. The
   debt collector is not going to take up a collection to
   keep you off the streets and well-fed if you lose your
   ability to earn income. That is your job. Even when you

are in debt. And this money may be the only you have access to recover and get back on track, in the worst-case scenario.

2. **Increase Income.** Auto-depositing 10% of your income into your retirement account (as the first "bill" you pay) is one way to increase income because that is money that you would have spent or given to the debt collector. Another way to increase income is to learn how to make your money make money while you sleep – through wise investing strategies. If you don't know Modern Portfolio Theory, annual rebalancing, how to avoid the bailouts, what's safe, how to get safe and how to add in hot industries, read the Stocks and Bonds sections in this book. You should also read *You Vs. Wall Street*, which discusses the strategies I used to become a #1 stock picker. Buy and hold investors lost money in the last decade. Modern Portfolio Theory with annual rebalancing is easy as a pie chart and worked fantastically through the Great Recession and the Dot Com Recession before that. It also outperformed the bull markets in between, and has earned more than 10% annualized in the New Millennium.

3. **Decrease Expenses.** Cutting out café lattes could make you cranky, but it won't make you rich. This is where you

have to be brave and make bold choices. You also need to differentiate between "good" debt and "bad" debt. Education is the highest correlating factor with income – so this is usually a good investment. (Learn more about this in the Thrive Budget section of this book.) Dressing the part for your career is important, too. On the other hand, a new car loses a lot of value the minute you drive it off of the lot. And buying too much home, or trying to hang on to one you really can't afford, may be one of the biggest reasons you are in debt.

4. **The Big Three: Housing, Transportation & Insurance.** When you are considering how to cut expenses, you must look at housing, transportation and insurance, which are the three most expensive things in the budget. Yes, you must get creative, and think well outside of the box (and the bind) that you are currently in. So, can you house-share? Downsize? If you are an empty nester, do you really still need four bedrooms and a pool, particularly if you'd rather be traveling? Can you take public transportation, or ride a bike, to and from work? Carpool? Is it time to buy a more fuel-efficient car? As for insurance, there is one important consideration that might help tremendously, directly below.

5. **Health Savings Accounts.** If you are a healthy person who never goes to the doctor and you have a low

deductible insurance plan, you are making the insurance company rich. In fact, you could purchase a high deductible plan, save money in your Health Savings Account to cover the deductible in the worst case scenario, take a tax write-off and invest the money in your Health Savings Account for a chance at even more gains. Learn more about Health Savings Accounts on the IRS.gov website. **This is an option that could save most healthy people thousands of dollars each year.**

6. **Debt Consolidation.** As FINRA.org (the Financial Regulatory Agency) reminds us, "Few money-management strategies pay off as well as, or with less risk than, paying off all high interest debt you may have." FINRA.org has excellent resources and ideas for reducing debt. When you secure new debt to pay off old debt (like tapping a lower-interest line of home equity credit), be sure that is a part of an entire, sound money makeover that includes increased income and decreased expenses (ala The Thrive Budget™). Otherwise, you'll find yourself in trouble again very soon.

7. **Credit Counseling.** The Federal Trade Commission warns consumers that credit counseling agencies, even those that claim they are non-profit, can "charge high

fees, which may be hidden, or urge consumers to make "voluntary" contributions that can cause more debt." So, rather than think this is a panacea, you must have your guard up. Loan modification scams were, sadly, plentiful, during the Great Recession – preying on the most desperate homeowners. For tips on how to get the best help, review the FTC.gov web page on debt. The strategies for reducing expenses and increasing income in this book are also key to developing a sustainable, long-term plan that puts you in the driver's seat, instead of "the man" – specifically the salesman, the tax man and the debt collector. There are more laws on your side than you may be aware of.

8. **Personal Bankruptcy: Chapter 7 and 13.** There are two chief differences between these two types of personal bankruptcy. You must wait 8 years to file Chapter 7 again; whereas you could file for Chapter 13 in two years. And if you have a steady income, you may be able to save your home and car in Chapter 13, whereas those assets have a higher likelihood of being repossessed in Chapter 7. Both may, in many cases, stop foreclosures, repossessions, utility shut-offs and debt collection, at least temporarily. (Which means no more calls from the debt collector. Woo hoo!!) There are fees involved in bankruptcy filings and **you must get credit counseling**

before any discharge will be granted. USCourts.gov/ BankruptcyCourts has additional information and forms. It's a good idea to read over the information to determine if this is a strategy that fits your situation. It's also a very good idea to hire a reputable, experienced attorney to guide you through the process and file the paperwork for you.

9. **The Thrive Budget**™. What will get you out of debt forever and put you on the path to financial freedom? Adopting a Thrive Budget, which is based on the simple theory of 50% to Thrive and 50% to Survive. When you limit your basic needs to 50% of your income (and yes, you can do this), then you have 50% to invest in things that increase your net worth, your social worth, your human capital (employability) and your fun factor (which promotes good health). I outline exactly how to do this in the section of the same name in this book.

10. **Financial Education.** I know economics majors who haven't the first clue about a sustainable household budget, or how to identify companies that are headed for bankruptcy. The U.S. wouldn't have any banks, if we hadn't bailed them out in 2007-2008. The average certified financial planner has hundreds of clients and is hired as a salesman (not an analyst or stock whiz). In

fact, almost everything you buy – from your home to your car to your insurance plan and mutual funds – is sold to you by a commissioned-based salesman. The turnover in the brokerage business, particularly on the front end, is extremely high – more so during recessions. Therefore, you cannot just blindly trust any "financial professional" to invest your money for you. It is time to learn the ABCs of Money and take responsibility of your financial future.

The 21st Century is very different from the 20th Century. The developed world is debt laden and in slow growth mode, while the developing world is expanding rapidly and concerned about inflation. And we are all linked together in a complicated web of interdependence.

Once you know basic financial literacy, you will never again be naïve about the average returns of real estate, stocks, bonds, gold, hard assets, etc. Wisdom can inform your "money while you sleep" passive income strategies, instead of blind faith. (You know that has burned you big time in the past.) You will know the hard truth behind the hard sale.

So, don't let fear of FICO score keep you trapped in the quicksand of debt. Once you adopt the *wealth consciousness* strategies that have helped the richest people in America pare their debt and manifest their dreams, the sky is the limit on what you can achieve.

If you are deeply in debt, then it may be time to use the laws of the land, and the plentiful free resources that are available from U.S. government agencies (if you look in the right place), to push the reset button. Once you file your paperwork for Chapter 7, 11 or 13, all of the calls from debt collectors end. It's in the court's hands. (So be sure you have good representation and follow all of the rules, which will determine whether or not you are successful in discharging your debt.) Throughout the process, keep putting 10% of your income (at least) into your tax-protected retirement plan.

If you are waiting to get out of debt before you start saving and investing, then you are making the debt collectors rich at your own expense. And you are reinforcing bad money habits. The game is rigged to trap you by compounding your debt; you can free yourself by compounding your gains.

Fiscal health is a lot like physical health. Eat right and exercise and those good daily habits go a long way to beautifying your bottom line. If you were binging and purging, whether it was with risky investment schemes that didn't pan out or just using your credit cards or the home equity ATM machine to fund an unsustainable lifestyle, then you need to deal with the excess weight and health issues that have come up, by adopting a healthier plan. Part of the change must include incorporating wisdom over blind faith, and bypassing the fast food joint (my metaphor for any get-rich-quick investment scheme).

Bottom Line

Most people who are in debt are making the debt collector rich, at the expense of themselves. Paying off your credit cards and getting out of debt require a game plan designed by you, not the debt collector, that considers the laws of the land and includes a healthier income and budgeting plan.

Take-Away Suggestions

1. If you are serious about paying off your credit cards, start by adopting the Thrive Budget, which includes increasing income, decreasing expenses and depositing 10% of your income *first* into a tax-protected retirement account *no matter what.*
2. Look at the big-ticket expenses – housing, transportation and insurance – first. Adopting a sustainable lifestyle most often includes downsizing in these three areas.

3. If you are healthy and paying an arm and a leg for health insurance, consider a Health Savings Account as a way of increasing income and decreasing your bills.

Chapter 2: Hello Freedom. Good-Bye Debt.

Debt is the biggest game out there. As I discussed in chapter one, credit card companies can lend money to you, and then charge you interest upon interest, compounding the original amount borrowed over and over again until you can't see beyond the wall of debt you owe. Then, they get to hound you daily until you set up a payment plan, and the calls are so incessant and threatening that many people are paying their debt FIRST before they address their own needs.

It's easy to be confused and afraid, when the debt collectors threaten to take you to court, get a judgment and put a lien on your income if you don't pay up monthly and stick with it, and that fear can rule your decision-making, if you let it. However, placing compounding debt as the master of your finances only ensures indentured servitude. Whereas paying yourself first, getting real about your income, assets and spending, and accessing the legal protections that are offered by the laws of the land are the only tickets to freedom.

It is your job, at all times, to ensure that your health savings accounts, retirement accounts, college funds and more – all investments that have a chance to compound returns *for you and your children* and increase *your family* income and assets – are your first priority.

Why?

Credit card companies use compounding to entrap people in the cycle of debt. Investors use the power of compounding to liberate themselves from the shackles of borrowing and overspending.

How can you possibly do this, when you are in debt and don't have even one extra thin dime?

You will have to address other areas of your income and expenses to get your budget in balance, as outlined in chapter one. But, just as importantly, you also have to shift your mindset, your goals, your habits and your *consciousness*. Investor *consciousness* means that you understand that your well being, your ability to earn income, is central to your ability to pay down debt in the first place. Think of "paying yourself first" as your seeds of prosperity. If you don't seed your fields, you'll never have enough to feed yourself. The debt collector is certainly not going to seed your fields for you, and the only harvest he is interested in is the one that comes at your expense.

The thinking that you should get out of debt *before* you start investing is flawed thinking. I already explained the importance of compounding your gains, increasing your passive income and protecting your assets in financial predator-proof retirement accounts. However, there is another reason why paying yourself first is critically important to fighting back. Debt and spending are nothing more than habits and your life underwater is an obsession with "not drowning" rather than "swimming."

Clearly, if you were as focused on income and passive income as you are on paying down debt, you'd be swimming in assets now, instead of drowning in debt. Saving and investing are also habits, and the sooner you focus on compounding returns, the sooner you'll have the income and assets needed to negotiate better terms on your debt, and protect your money from debt collection and liens. You will also shift out of the habit of borrowing and spending more than you earn, which was obviously completely out of control when you suffered from debt consciousness.

Compounding Gains and Increased Assets

Here's how powerful compounding your gains is. If you simply save $4,000/year for 30 years, at the end of that time, you have saved $120,000. If you *invest* $4,000/year for 30 years and that earns 10% annualized (what stocks and bonds have done for the past 30 years), then you will amass $723,776. By year 40, your nest egg will be worth over $2 million. In short, compounding your investment gains is your ticket to freedom!

	IRA Annual Deposit	10% Gains	Total
Year 1	$4,000	$400	$4,400
Year 5	$4,000	$2,442	$26,862
Year 10	$4,000	$6,375	$70,124
Year 15	$4,000	$12,709	$139,798
Year 20	$4,000	$22,910	$252,010
Year 25	$4,000	$39,339	$432,728
Year 30	$4,000	$65,798	$723,776
Year 35	$4,000	$132,015	$1,316.148
Year 40	$4,000	$195,140	$2,146.532
TOTAL	$160,000	$1,986,532	$2,146,532

Again, here's another way to think of it. If you invest 10% of your income and that earns a 10% gain each year, you'll have more money than you earn within seven years and your money will make more than you do within 25 years. Investment therapy will make you far happier than retail therapy (which makes the credit card companies very happy)! And if you start at the age of 20, you're ready to retire by 45. (If you started using credit cards at 20, you're likely still in debt at 45, saying that you'll start investing when you get out of debt.)

If you are drowning in debt and signing over your income to the credit card companies each month, you can't blame the credit card companies. All they want is your money. Taking your money is their job. It's not their job to advise you on what is the most sound financial plan for you. The best plan for them keeps you:

1. Making minimum payments (so that the interest and penalties compound and your debt balloons)

2. Does not improve your FICO score (the compounded debt means that you could have more debt than assets, which prevents you from qualifying for other credit cards and loans – and keeps you paying them first),

3. Paying the debt collector first (before your own livelihood, retirement and medical), often,

4. Places you even more at risk for personal bankruptcy.

If you are in trouble on your mortgage, the bank can foreclose and resell the property to a new borrower, keeping all of the money you paid to them. (They win either way.) If the bank and credit card company are charging you a high interest rate or penalties, the amount you owe may be increasing exponentially, even as you attempt to "pay it down." And as long as you keep paying monthly, without negotiating better terms or setting up a Debt Management Plan, the penalties, compounding and fees keep increasing and increasing until you declare bankruptcy or give them double, triple or even ten times the amount you originally borrowed.

Meanwhile, you assume that since you're making your payments timely, your FICO score is improving. Now you know that your credit score has gone into the toilet because you owe too much. And you probably also assumed that the credit card company would be so happy with your timely payments that they would strike a good settlement with you when you have the extra dough to strike a deal (which you haven't even been amassing). In fact, if you falter in the least, the debt collector will seek a judgment against you for the full amount, including fees, compounding and interest, as quickly as possible to get a judgment and file a lien against your income and unprotected assets, putting them first in line before the other people you owe money to.

If you are spending all your income and draining your retirement plan and assets to pay the debt collector, you better pray that nothing happens to you because the debt collector is not going to take up a collection for you if you lose your job, or are forced to retire, or have a health issue arise, or lose your home. So, if you're not funding your own retirement plan and health savings account first – before you pay the bill collectors – you are literally sinking your own lifeboat. (As I said in chapter one, money in qualified retirement plans is yours to keep no matter what.)

That is why it is so important to have reason and sound strategies ruling your lifestyle, rather than fear of the debt collector's next call.

Here's what has to change. You have to shift out of debtor and spender consciousness and into investor consciousness. And as you start changing your thoughts, your actions have to change, too. You'll have to replace all of the thoughts and actions that didn't work, with sound strategies that have stood the test of time.

The Hello Freedom! Mindset

The Hello Freedom! Mindset means that you will use the Thrive Budget, limiting your basic needs expenditures to 50%, so that you have 50% left to thrive on. You will invest, rather than spend. You will separate work accounts and money from personal life. You will course correct when you make a mistake. You will use a qualified counselor to help you set up a Debt Management Plan, if that is the best way to reduce your indebtedness. And you will consider the possibility of foreclosure and bankruptcy, if your debts are eating you out of house, retirement and home. (Remember how quickly Rupert Murdoch, the chairman and CEO of News Corp., closed down *News of the World* during the phone hacking scandals?) You will verify, analyze and put everything in writing. You will consider this more important than your job because the only way out of the rat race is to get rid of your high-interest debt and activate your money while you sleep investments. Your job's income stops the minute you can't work.

Debtors and spenders focus on paying down debt before increasing their assets. They spend more than they earn. They have blind faith in the integrity of others. They think that working harder and earning more income will solve the problem. If the accountant or money manager or business manager or partner makes bad choices and loses too much money, they may feel like a victim and whine about it. They also may justify everything saying that it was bad economic conditions. Or who could have predicted the Great Recession. (Ahem! I alerted investors to overweight safe from the Great Recession in January of 2008, when the Dow Jones Industrial Average was still trading above 13,000, and I wasn't the only one to do so.)

The Hello Freedom! person never relies on blind faith, and understands, approves and takes responsibility for the actions of the people who work for her. Investors know that sound strategies and predictable returns on investments create financial freedom whereas having blind faith in others to do everything for them is a losing, high risk game. (Madoff is only one example of this.)

Which one are you? Take a look at the various areas below and rank yourself as having the Hello Freedom! mindset and skill set or that of the Debtor or the Spender.

1. **Money Habits**: Do you pay 10% into your IRA and 401K as the first thing you do when income arrives? Or do you pay the debt collector first before any other consideration? Do you spend all of your money trying to make your small business profitable as the only priority?

2. **Money Mindset**: Do you focus on increasing your assets and your return on investments through smart strategies, in addition to earning a good income? Or are you hyper focused on improving your FICO score and keeping the debt collectors happy? Or do you spend most of your time and money networking in local meetings and attending marketing seminars to try and drum up more business?

3. **Plan for Escaping the Rat Race and Living the Rich Life**: Have you adopted the Thrive Budget, Modern Portfolio Theory, easy-as-a-pie chart nest egg strategies and the 3-Ingredient Recipe for Cooking Up Profits? Or are you clinging onto investments that have lost value, praying for a Hail Mary miracle that erases your losses and achieves unbelievable gains, and borrowing money

to stay afloat in the meantime? Are you so afraid of the idea of investing that you invest only in yourself and your business, but get tempted to buy gold because that's what everyone else is doing?

4. **Health, Health Insurance and Health Savings Accounts**: Do you have a high deductible with a health savings account that you manage for 10% ROI? Or, are you stressed out all of the time, worried about your health, angry at all of the ways you are being eaten alive by bills, and paying an arm and a leg for health insurance because you *have to*? Or, do you spend most of your "extra" money on fun and pleasure instead of health insurance? Are you uninsured?

5. **Outlook on Business**: Do you work hard, course correct, adopt best business practices and keep work and family and home life separate? Or are you so worried about your finances that you are crabby with your family and draining your life savings to try and hang onto everything, including a failing business or investment? Have you borrowed from family and friends to buy another self-help seminar or online marketing course?

6. **Outlook on Life:** Do you take responsibility for your fiscal health? Or do you feel like a victim? Or are you

just perplexed as to why all of your Law of Attraction seminars ended up costing you so much money, instead of bringing the riches they promised?

Once you understand how your thinking has trapped you in a cycle of over-spending and debt, you can start planning and acting more like an investor who is taking ownership of her life and is determined to get financially free. You will shift out of debt consciousness and into prosperity and abundance. Out of victim mentality and into ownership. Out of trying to appease the credit card companies, banks, debt collectors and others who hound you for a payment, and into a workable Debt Management Plan that allows you to contribute to your own Retirement Plan and basic needs, while you pay off debt on the best possible terms. You will transform out of depression, disgust, rage and/or helplessness into being a conscious creator of your world and our world at large.

Bottom Line

There are all kinds of ways that people get into debt, but all of these ways stem from the same mind traps, financial predatory scams and fiscally unhealthy actions. By adopting the mindset and daily habits of a savvy, confidant owner/investor, you will say Good-Bye to Debt and Hello to Freedom. In short, you must invest in yourself and in your future FIRST. There is no debt reduction plan without income. After earned income, then determine the best course to increase your passive income (including return on investments). Once you have income (earned and passive), then you can pay down your debt faster and more easily, prioritizing your high-interest "bad" debt first, and get your spending under control.

Take-Away Suggestions

1. Determine whether you have an investor, a debtor or a spender's consciousness. Use the chart above to help you adopt a healthier frame of mind.

2. Debtors and spenders both suffer from "lack" mentality, though they look very different. Debtors are distressed and worried, and have no faith in the system, though they hope for a Hail Mary solution. Spenders are magical, spiritual and have all the faith in the world — slathered on top of a nagging fear of failure in their gut.

3. In addition to depositing 10% of your income into a tax-protected retirement account, first, before anything else, commit to selecting a charity to donate 10% of your income to for the next year. If you cannot justify the money, then donate the *time*. This will assist you in getting into the "I have more than enough to give"

mindset. (Don't over give here. 10% is sustainable. More than that is part of the same old distracted, magical thinking that got you into trouble in the first place.)

4. When adopting new habits, remember that they will feel *uncomfortable*. The habits that contributed to where you are now are comfortable, but flawed. The solutions that will get you out of this mess are new, unfamiliar and uncomfortable – but they work.

Chapter 3: Buyer Beware: Good Debt vs. Bad Debt.

When I think of life in today's world, the thing that comes to mind is "Buyer Beware." You are sold a house, a car, insurance, shoes, clothes, medicine, investments... Everything you think you need to survive and thrive is *sold* to you. Most of the time by someone who benefits from the sale, whether it is a commission, a bonus, a promotion, or just the fact that you become a regular customer.

Imagine how much different your life would be if you knew that every time you stepped out your door, someone, many times calling themselves an "expert," had something to sell you. When you go to buy a car, the salesman, who is paid on commission, will try to sell you the most expensive car s/he can. When you go to buy a home, the realtor will show you homes more expensive than you can afford. A few years ago, a creative mortgage broker would have designed a loan for you that made you *think* you could afford an expensive home, even if you couldn't. All of these "experts" are commission-based salesmen, trained and hired to sell you things. And their own livelihood depends upon them selling you as much as they can.

Absolutely no one is thinking of your budget, or how his or her sale fits into the big picture of what you can really afford. So, if you aren't adding everything up and making sound choices on the big-ticket items, you'll be drowning in credit card debt in no time at all. Most people are spending far too much on their housing, car, food, insurance, etc. – their basic needs. When you are struggling to survive, buried alive in bills, you are not able to enjoy life. The Thrive Budget™ gives you time, money and permission to have fun, be charitable, educate yourself and invest for additional passive income while you sleep – all of the things that make life more enjoyable.

But the sales don't stop there. The shoe salesman. The clothing salesman. The seminars. The newsletters. The TV ads. The nonprofit you donated to 25 years ago that still calls you every Christmas. Once, at a fish shop, the guy behind the counter actually tried to sell me a 25-pound fish! The twenty-something girl at the waxing salon just tried to convince me that nostril waxing is the latest fad and that it is healthy because it helps your allergies.

But the sales don't stop there. The scare ads that tell you America is going to hell in a hand basket and only buying gold or electing a fiscal conservative President will fix it. (Congress controls the budget and taxes, not the President, however the President can start two wars, like President Bush did.) The "friend" who has a sure shot oil investment opportunity in Texas, where the studies were leaked (only to them) by Exxon Mobil (and there is no mention of whether that is actually legal)...

You are sold prescriptions to lower your blood pressure, to lower your cholesterol and to increase your blood flow. In fact, the best path to health – to lower blood pressure, lower cholesterol and increase blood flow – is to eat right and exercise (particularly in a nation where 1/3 of our citizens are obese). I was at a women's health conference where none of the female doctors mentioned diet and exercise as an efficacious tool for the afore-mentioned – until one of the laywomen in the room stood up and asked why this had been overlooked.

As one personal example of this: my son's pediatrician used to joke that he did his job too well. He only saw my son during well child checkups! The pediatrician I was using only one year prior to finding Dr. Jay Gordon lost her job when she prescribed year-round antibiotics to treat my son's recurring ear infections. Dr. Jay's pro-immune system, anti-allergy approach cured the problem in three short months, and promoted health so well that my son never got sick again!

In today's world, you cannot afford to rely *solely* on the experts. You must understand that good habits are as important to fiscal health as they are to physical health.

Assume that everyone is a salesman and everyone has skin in the game that they are advising you to play.

Below are a few more examples of "expert" advice gone awry:

1. **Gold Coins:** In 2010-2011, there was a popular cable commentator who was scaring people into buying gold coins that would have to increase in value 55% in order for investors to break even on their purchase. On February 22, 2012, Goldline (the company touted endlessly by this host on his former television program) settled with the City of Santa Monica, California (where the company is based) and agreed to pay $5.3 million in restitution to clients. Goldline was forced to stop using deceptive sales tactics, to provide more information and disclosures to clients and to submit to ongoing monitoring at its own expense. In exchange, the City of Santa Monica dismissed criminal charges against the company. The commentator lost his TV show ten months before the settlement was reached.

2. **Facebook, Groupon and Zynga IPOs.** To gaming and social network junkies, these were massively popular companies that were finally going public! When I crunched the numbers, I warned that these were Silicon Valley Spinster IPOs designed to marry off cash

negative companies to unsuspecting investors, so that insiders could profit.

3. **Blue Chips**. The leading blue chip index turned out to be the leading bailout index during the Great Recession, when six out of 30 companies were bailed out or went bankrupt (namely General Motors, AIG, Citigroup, Bank of America, American Express and JP Morgan Chase). That is 20%! Even today, the companies paying the highest dividends are those with the highest debt. This is why, "New Chips are Safer Than Blue Chips." Learn more in the chapter of the same name.

4. **Bonds and Credit Risk**. I first warned about bonds in 2008, before the Portugal, Ireland, Italy, Greece and Spain bond crisis (which put MF Global into bankruptcy). Bond investors have been falsely lured into a sense of safety with the Fed's promise to keep interest rates low until 2015. However, the bond market is being driven by *credit risk*, not interest rate risk. (Interest rates are rock bottom in Europe, but that hasn't stopped the PIIGS bond crisis there.) If you think that any legacy company is immune to the debt problems of its industry, remember that American Airlines managed to stay afloat for years, while all of its competitors went bankrupt. American Airlines filed for

Chapter 11 in November 2011, and was still struggling to put deals into place that would allow it to re-emerge from bankruptcy a year later.

5. **Saving Your Home.** Homeowners have been trying to hang on since the onset of the Great Recession, but that hasn't stopped over 12 million properties from entering the foreclosure process (between 2007 and 2012). More than two million foreclosures were initiated by banks in 2012, and there is more to come in 2013. So, rather than let the bank design a plan to save your home (which will always be designed to benefit them), or ignore the problem (which festers) it's a good idea to get help now from independent sources that have no skin in the game. Never tap your retirement plans to keep a home you really can't afford. What you need is a full budget analysis and a sound, long-term strategy that makes fiscal sense for you (not just your bank and their debt collection sales team). Learn more about the legal options that are available to you in the real estate section of this book. Even if you have been denied a loan modification and have received a foreclosure notice, there is a way to keep all of your retirement money, *and* stay in your home, *and* (finally) get that loan modification you've been begging and pleading with the bank to sign off on.

No matter who is trying to "help" you, you cannot simply have blind faith. The only thing you can trust these days is *results* – over a 10-year period.

Here are a few more examples of "expert" financial advice gone awry.

1. **Seeking Investment Advice from an Accountant.** A friend received investment advice from her accountant – to pull money out of her home and invest it in high yield 3rd trust deeds. She didn't understand the risk and lost all of her money – which she still owed, with interest, to the bank. The accountant received a "finder's fee" for referring her, but didn't lift a finger to help her recover the principal. When my friend threatened to sue, the accountant and the company with the thirds declared bankruptcy.

2. **No One Cares About Your Money More Than You Do.** In 2000, a retired autoworker accepted a lump sum instead of a pension. He then lost almost all of it in the NASDAQ crash – on Internet stocks a broker, who had been referred by the auto manufacturer, recommended. Modern Portfolio Theory is actually the most respected investment strategy. According to my pie charts, less than 5% of the retiree's pension should have been

invested in NASDAQ, which would have meant that more than 95% would have been protected from losses.

3. **New Chips are Safer Than Blue Chips.** A financial professional purchased foolproof Lehman Bros. preferred stock for his retired father (and you know what happened there). Being in business for over a century doesn't guarantee you'll keep the lights on tomorrow.

4. **Get Rich Quick Scheme Designed by a Commission-Based Realtor.** A single guy decided to pull equity out of his home and purchase three homes in Vegas in 2006. Instead of owning a valuable home free and clear, he lost all of his properties. Another couple was advised to buy a beach house in 2006 by a *close relative*, who was a realtor and made commission on the deal. They rented the house for about half of their annual costs, and the home itself lost more than 25% of its value.

The events appear to be different, but the underlying problem is the same – having blind faith in a commission-based salesman. (In each of the above situations, the salesman made a commission.) As TD AMERITRADE chairman Joe Moglia tells us, ""Nobody cares more about your money than you do."

The other commonality is that many of these are "bad debt" transactions. In general, any time you borrow money, you want the future to be guaranteed of being brighter than today. When you buy a new car, you lose a lot of value when you drive the car off the lot. Why not consider purchasing a low-mileage car that is a couple of years old?

When you borrow money to buy a home in the hopes of buying it and flipping it, you are only guaranteed a brighter tomorrow if real estate is in a bull market, the remodel gets done on time and on budget and buyers like your neighborhood and home. There are a lot of ifs in that sentence. If that is not the case, you could be stuck with an illiquid, underwater asset, which is exactly what happened for over twelve million people (so far) since the Great Recession.

Good Debt vs. Bad Debt

I can make a better case for clothes – particularly for a good business wardrobe – within reason. You must look the part if you want the job. However, are you just using retail therapy whenever you feel bad? Are you a shopaholic?

Education is the highest correlating factor with income – so an investment in education is good debt that almost always pays off. There are a few degrees, particularly in The Arts, that can be hit or miss, simply because artists throughout history have been notoriously underpaid – even the uber-famous ones, like Van Gogh, Oscar Wilde, Mozart, Maya Angelou and Kate Winslet, who received a salary equivalent to a rounding error of the almost $2 billion in profits of *Titanic*. Almost everyone with a computer science or engineering degree is working, even today. In fact, there are over three million unfilled jobs, mostly in STEM fields, science, technology, engineering and math, even while there is still 7.9% unemployment.

Doctors end up with $250,000 (or more) in student loans, but also make $170,000-$250,000 a year (source: Bureau of Labor Statistics, 2011). Computer programmers are earning $76,000/year. People without a high school diploma make less than $24,000/year, on average, and had an unemployment rate of 14% – double the national average – in 2011. Uneducated Americans were 5.6 times more likely to be without a job than those with a professional or doctoral degree in 2011. Unemployment in the educated American population was only 2.5%. I'll discuss this more in the chapter on the Thrive Budget, when we discuss why you want to set aside 10% of your income for education.

Education Pays

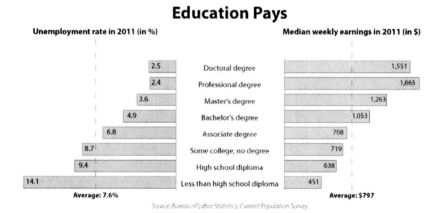

Unemployment rate in 2011 (in %)		Median weekly earnings in 2011 (in $)
2.5	Doctoral degree	1,551
2.4	Professional degree	1,665
3.6	Master's degree	1,263
4.9	Bachelor's degree	1,053
6.8	Associate degree	768
8.7	Some college, no degree	719
9.4	High school diploma	638
14.1	Less than high school diploma	451
Average: 7.6%		Average: $797

Source: Bureau of Labor Statistics, Current Population Survey

Education also pays when it comes to the ABCs of Money. It is far more important that you understand the Thrive Budget, the 3-Ingredient Recipe for Cooking Up Profits, the Four Questions for Picking a Winning Company, easy-as-a-pie chart nest egg strategies, Modern Portfolio Theory, the average annual returns of real estate, stocks, bonds, gold, hard assets and more, than it is that you can calculate the difference between a train going 30 MPH compared to one going 15.6 MPH between Buffalo and DC. You don't have to hammer every nail in your money house. You can still hire someone to manage it if you wish. But if you are the architect of your dream life, then you can set people straight, with confidence, when they are going off the blueprint.

Once you get the basic financial literacy training that you should have received in high school, you can discern a good investment from a money pit and a good financial partner from … a salesman. Once you know how to combine common sense with reliable data and simple math skills, you'll never be vulnerable again.

A great MD can't get you walking and a great financial advisor can't keep you from buying a bigger house or car than you can afford. A great contractor can't build you a house, if you don't know how many bedrooms and bathrooms you need.

I've seen an office administrator and a handyman save their nest egg, earn gains during the Great Recession and make 40% gains the first time they invested in a single company stock. I've seen a young family retool their living situation, so that they could afford investing in their child's college fund, in addition to diapers. I've seen an educator create the means to take two 30-day love excursions with her husband, during a time when most people were cutting all of the fun out of their wallet. I've even seen a retired policymaker learn investing from the billionaire Warren Buffett (by investing in Berkshire Hathaway and religiously reading his updates and attending his annual meetings).

It's time to get the ABCs of Money that you should have received in high school. So that you never fall victim to a bad deal again. So that you can join this growing list of people who are making wise choices in their income, their budgeting and their passive income. The result is a solid financial foundation to support the life of your dreams.

Bottom Line

Buyer: beware.

Informed consumer and investor: be empowered.

Thrive Budget™ adopter: step into the life of your dreams.

Take-Away Suggestions

1. Remember that almost every "expert" you deal with is hired to sell you something. Know what you want and how much you are willing to spend before you walk into the store or make the call.

2. There is a big difference between good debt (like education) and bad debt (like retail therapy).

3. Education is the highest correlating factor with income. It is also important to getting a job in America in this century.

Part 2: Real Estate

Chapter 4: Got Real Estate Problems? 6 Case Study Solutions.

Real Estate prices are at a 10-year low (nationwide, on average) and mortgage rates are at a lifetime low. That creates a fantastic opportunity to purchase a new home.

The trouble is that:

1. Many people are underwater, breaking their budget to pay their mortgages and just trying to hang on. Some are burning through their retirement plans... (A no-no in almost every scenario.)

2. Some people gave their home back (through short sale, foreclosure or bankruptcy) and have a lousy credit score.

3. Some people have a lot of cash on the sidelines but feel they might be trying to catch a falling knife. Who knows when real estate prices will bottom out?

4. Some people would rather drink mud than rent to someone. Some cities have such tight rent control standards that you could be stuck with a litigious tenant, or a destructive tenant, who costs you far more than you could earn in rental income.

5. Be careful of loaning money to someone so that they can stay in their current home. You might not be helping the situation at all. With a carefully constructed strategy, your "help" could be secured and also provide the long-term strategy that pays off for everyone, instead of trying to buy an extremely short-term fix that makes everyone, except the bank, a loser.

Below are a few case studies to show you a different way of thinking. These people all found a way out of the tight squeeze that many people are experiencing with real estate, and into a far better situation. Since the Mortgage Debt Relief Act is set to expire in December of 2012 (but might be renewed for another year or two), the clock is ticking on how much support you might receive from the federal government.

Case Study 1: Young professional father with two children had to move to a different city for work. His home was underwater, but not by a lot. Still he couldn't sell it without a short sale.

Option A: Staying Put

This was not an option for him because he had to move for his work. He could not have kept the house and rented it because his costs were higher than the rent level. With a young family, that was simply unaffordable. His mortgage had reset to a very high interest rate.

Option B: Purchasing a New Home

This was a few years ago, and YPF negotiated with the bank to give the property back in a Deed In Lieu transaction. When he moved to the new city, he became a renter. He thought his credit was shot and that buying again was out of the question – until he began speaking to his parents. They had a lot of money on the side that was earning zero percent interest. His parents agreed to purchase the home he was renting. They gave him a lease/option, applying a percentage of his rent to a down payment fund, so that in a few years when his credit recovers, he can purchase the house from them. In the meantime, his parents make a little extra income, which helps them pay their own bills, and is far above what they'd receive from any other "safe" investment – at 7%. Even with this interest rate, the father's rent is reasonable.

Case Study 2: Single professional has a home purchased for $158,000 that is worth only $100,000 today, but has a low interest rate.

Option A: Staying Put

This single professional woman with a good income for her city has a reasonably low-interest rate mortgage, but is underwater (i.e. the value of her property is worth $50,000 less than her $150,000 mortgage). Based upon an average real estate return of 5% annually, it could take 10 years for her home to recover its value. Her home would be basically unsellable during that 10-year period, unless she executed a "short sale." She is concerned because if the bank "forgives" the $50,000 debt in a short sale, it creates taxable "phantom" income. So, even though SPW wants to move to be with her fiancée (who lives in a different city) and start a family, she thought she was stuck with the house. Fortunately, right now, there is a Mortgage Debt Forgiveness Act, which forgives debt incurred on her primary residence. This Act is set to expire in 2012, but may be extended to 2013 or beyond. The other option, if the bank will agree to it, is to give the home back to the bank in a deed in lieu. Renting the home would not cover her expenses, and managing the property would be difficult for her, given that she already works 70-hour weeks and would live in a different city. It's a university town, so she's also afraid the frat boys will cost a lot in maintenance.

Option B: Purchasing a New Home

The couple purchased a new family home together as co-owners, in the fiancé's city. *After* they purchased their new home together, they worked with the bank on a deed in lieu. Now, instead of having a decade of living apart, being underwater on a mortgage and trying to crawl back to even, they are starting their family together in a home that could increase $55,000 or more over the next decade. The bank is happy with the deed in lieu because it is trying to stabilize prices in the neighborhood. No phantom income was created (and if it was, it would not have been taxable, thanks to the Mortgage Relief Act).

Case Study 3: Young married mother has a home she purchased while single at the top of the market for $250,000. Its value today is $80,000, but she has a fixed, low interest rate for 30 years. Her husband is the "owner" of their family home, and she has been renting out "her home" (while keeping a small sanctuary/office there). She is $300-$400/month out of pocket, when you factor in taxes, mortgage, insurance and upkeep.

Option A: Staying Put

This young mother could be underwater for 25 years, based upon average real estate returns of 5% annually. She could be paying $3600-$4800 annually throughout that period of time – $100,000 or more in expenses – without any ability to recoup or stop those losses by selling the home. A quarter of a century is a long time to be stuck with an illiquid, underwater investment. That's longer than she'll be financially responsible for her child!

Option B: Purchasing a New Home

She purchased a second home (with her husband) with a low fixed interest rate at market value, and rented that out to the same person who is living in her home now. Then she made $500/month profit (instead of being $300-$400/month in the hole). In 25 years, the new home could be worth $260,000, which is $180,000 more than the purchase price. When/if they wish to sell they make a fantastic profit (instead of having two decades of being illiquid and trying to crawl back to even). She did not qualify for a deed in lieu because the property is underwater too much. The bank resold the first home at market rate through the "short sale" process. There were no taxes due, however, thanks to the Mortgage Debt Forgiveness Act. Because she got rid of a huge debt – owing $180,000 more than her home was worth – her credit rating actually improved.

Case Study 4: A single professional has two properties that were purchased in 2008. Both properties have lost some value, but are only underwater about 15%. He has variable interest rate loans on both properties that are currently set at under 3%! His rental income gives him about $500/month. His worry is that interest rates will rise significantly and fast in a few years, and then he'll be in trouble. He can't lock in a fixed rate because he's underwater on the mortgage (though not significantly).

Option A: Staying Put

Here's another case where calling in friends and family solved the problem. This man's parents were retired and worried about having too much money riding the Wall Street Rollercoaster. When he approached them with the offer that they purchase the homes with cash in two years, and "sell" them back to him at a 6% interest rate – secured by the properties – they were happy to do so! The deals have been drafted, with the help of attorneys and accountants, and are just waiting for the winds to shift in interest rates.

Option B: Purchasing a New Home

In this case, property values have not come down enough to make it advantageous to buy something new. The only real problem was making sure he wouldn't be stuck in a double-digit interest rate, if the U.S. experiences inflation and a steep rise in interest rates going forward. That was solved with bringing in a partner, and the partner was protected by making the loan an official document, secured by the property in case of default on payment.

Case Study 5: A retired couple owns their home free and clear. They live in a sunny state with extreme highs in the summer and lows in the winter, and are interested in putting up solar panels to take their energy bills down to

zero. They desire to take out a low-interest rate equity loan (under 4%) to do this.

Option A: Staying Put

The prices on solar panels have come down dramatically over the last few years, to the point that the payback time can be 4-7 years for people living in sunny states (using the available tax subsidies). It is easy to connect to the grid in their neighborhood, which means that during the day, when demand for energy and prices are high, they sell energy to the grid and at night, when the sun isn't shining, they are able to draw energy back from the grid without any fees. The cost of the solar system and installation will be paid back in 4-7 years, and then they have free energy for life!

Option B: Purchasing a New Home

This couple is not comfortable with being landlords. (They lost money trying to save a home for a friend. A bad move, unless you have a great strategy first!) So, the best option for them was taking advantage of their ability to borrow money at 3% interest, purchase solar panels that cost less than half of what they did a few years ago, enjoy tax deductions and ensure that they save more than $3000 a year on their energy bill for the rest of their life!

Case Study 6: Middle-Aged Bachelor who loves to travel built a custom, manufactured home in a unique beachfront

community. He had problems with the construction, which created discord in the community. When he returns home from his travels, he feels ostracized from his neighbors – not exactly the beach bliss he had envisioned. To compound the matter, he borrowed $500,000 to build his place, and other similar homes in the community are selling for closer to $225,000 in short sales, foreclosures, etc. He has a fixed, low interest rate (4.1%).

Option A: Staying Put

He could be underwater for 17 years, based upon average real estate returns of 5% annually.

Option B: Purchasing a New Home

This particular bachelor loves Las Vegas! He could purchase an iconic mid-century modern home in Las Vegas for half the price that he owes on his construction nightmare. Meanwhile, a new owner would be more welcome in the community by the other homeowners (who could forgive him/her of the mistakes of the bachelor owner/builder). Instead of waiting 17 years for the value of his beach home to potentially return. He could partner with a friend/family member on purchasing a new home in Las Vegas for $225,000, in a great community (with them co-signing a loan for him). Alternatively, he could purchase two homes – at $115,000 each, and rent one of the homes out for a profit of $400-$500 monthly. Those homes have the potential to double (or more) in value over the next 17 years. What a better scenario than being ostracized and underwater by a quarter of a million dollars over the next two decades. In 17 years, this bachelor will in his late 60s – ready to retire. *After* buying the new Vegas homes, he can resale his beach house at market rate through a "short sale" process, just as other homeowners have done in the same community. There is no taxable income for the bachelor, if the Mortgage Debt Forgiveness Act is extended through 2013. And even if there was a taxable event, this might be far more affordable and advantageous than staying in the current home for the next two decades, and owing a quarter of a million dollars.

If you want to learn more about taxable phantom income and the Mortgage Debt Forgiveness Act, go to IRS.gov and/or ask your accountant.

From Drowning in Debt to King of the Hill!

When we think of the billionaire Donald Trump, we think of *The Apprentice* and his marquise properties in NYC and Florida (and more). However, Trump has had more real estate troubles than any of us. He was worth $2.9 billion in 2012, according to *Forbes*, but his company, Trump Hotels and Casino Resorts – now Trump Entertainment Resorts – has filed for bankruptcy multiple times. In other words, one of the keys to getting through this difficult time is not letting it *define* you. To Trump, he was just using the laws of the land to pare debt, and, unless you want to be indebted, illiquid and underwater for decades to come, you need to adopt this mindset, too.

The key here is that no one can do this on their own – in their own little cocoon. Sticking your head in the sand or seeking advice from the companies you are indebted to will only keep you sinking deeper and deeper in a bad situation. (They will design a plan that works best for them – at your expense.) If you are in trouble, it's time to get creative and to reach out to experts who can advise you on the law, tax implications and the real value of your home.

Bottom Line

The case studies above illustrate that everyone has their own story. Each person has her own unique situation, capabilities and problems. Each case requires some custom thinking. Your case will be different than any of these, but it shows you how to think creatively and keep your hopes up about finding a solution to your problem.

Take-Away Suggestions

1. What is the truth about the potential for your current real estate holdings to be something that buries you for the next two decades? Do a sober analysis based on where the market is headed now (from experts, not wishful thinking) and the average return of 5% annually in real estate.

2. Where will you be – in terms of age, your family and your career – in the one or two decades that it could take for the value of your property to return? Design a solution that positions you best in that time frame. (The bank is definitely doing that for their business. And if they are not, then they shouldn't be in business any way.)

3. Use sound, out-of-the-box thinking, expert accounting and bankruptcy counsel, legal options, sober projections and soul-searching to determine how to extricate yourself from a real estate nightmare. In most cases, that's time and money better spent than hounding your bank to give you a loan modification.

If you would like prosperity coaching to help think outside the box, call 310-430-2397 or visit NataliePace.com to learn more about my 3-day Investor Educational Retreats.

Chapter 5: Should You Do the Unthinkable?

Are you making the debt collectors and credit card companies rich on their compounding interest, while you bankrupt yourself? Should you short sale, foreclose, declare bankruptcy or hang on?

Now that you know the truth about your credit score, you should look at your debt with a more sober eye. Below we'll deal with being upside down on your mortgage. There are two main considerations if you owe significantly more than the value of your property.

Is this your home or is this income property?

One is personal and the other is strictly business.

If this is your home, then your cost/benefit analysis will include the following:

1. Do you love this home? Is it your sanctuary?
2. Is paying the mortgage cheaper than renting the same home?
3. Are you benefiting from the mortgage interest deduction?
4. Should you be downsizing any way?

5. Is there a chance that you might need to move for work or for any other reason before your home gains back its value?

6. Will having to pay tax on "phantom income" break your bank?

And here are a few different ways of answering these questions with a sober eye (rather than keeping your head stuck in the sand):

1. **Do you love this home?** Is it your sanctuary? If you've put a lot of extras in that mean a lot to you, factor this in. If this is a home with a lot of family history, or on land that has been in the family for generations, that will be important, too.

2. **Is paying the mortgage cheaper than renting the same home?** In many real estate markets in the United States, it is much cheaper to buy than it is to rent – at today's prices. However, if you purchased a few years ago, you are probably paying a lot more than market value.

3. **Are you benefiting from the mortgage interest deduction?** If this is your primary home and you earn a good income, this is another reason to stay a homeowner, rather than becoming a renter – particularly if some of the other answers on this list are "yes".

4. **Should you be downsizing any way?** A lot of Americans were tapping the home equity ATM machine before the real estate crash trying to stay in a home and lifestyle that they really couldn't afford. The most important thing you can do to cure your money ailments is to get your big-ticket basic needs spending within 50% of your income.

5. **Is there a chance that you might need to move for work or for any other reason before your home gains back its value?** Real estate is an illiquid asset and if you are deeply underwater on your mortgage, you could be stuck for decades to come. You won't be able to sell your home at the price you paid until the market value returns. Average annual real estate returns are less than 5%. If your $250,000 home is worth only $80,000 now, it could take 24 years for the value to return. Are you sure you want to spend the next quarter of a century living where you are? Can you really afford to be stuck where you are for the amount of time that it will take your home to regain its value?

6. **Will having to pay tax on "phantom income" break your bank?** During the tax years 2007-2012, the Mortgage Forgiveness Debt Relief Act allowed homeowners to exclude up to $2 million of debt

forgiven on their principal residence. Normally, debt forgiveness results in taxable income. So be sure to research on IRS.gov or with your accountant to find out if the Act has been extended and for how long, and if your situation applies.

If you are planning on living in this home for the rest of your life, and the mortgage payments are within your budget, and the mortgage, insurance and maintenance are less expensive than you could rent a home for, and you are benefitting from the mortgage interest rate deduction on your taxes, and the taxable income would create a real hardship for you, then hanging on might be a great idea. If you give the home back to the bank, then you may have to wait 5-7 years (or longer) before you can buy another house (unless you can pay cash for it or find alternative capital from friends and family). Once you factor in that you'll be paying a lot more in taxes as a renter (when you lose the mortgage interest write-off), you might not be saving anything at all by giving your home back to the bank. If you determine that keeping your home is the best idea, then lock in a fixed, low-interest rate loan (any way that you can) and enjoy your home. Also, file for a reassessment of the property value, so that you can reduce your property tax.

If your home is more than you can afford, and you are tapping every amount of income you've got (including your retirement accounts), and taking on expensive, compounding credit card debt to stay in it, then you must sober up and start looking at ways of adopting a more sustainable budget and lifestyle. The "unthinkable" is not the only solution. Can you rent out this expensive home and cover your costs, while you move into a more affordable place? If the answer is yes, and you're willing to be a landlord, then you might have found a viable solution, which provides some extra income for you. If you are just managing the property for the bank, and at risk of having more expense if the renter is hard on the property, then that's a pretty raw deal.

Can you hang on and sell the home for a profit in a few years? Should you get a new home and offer a deed in lieu to the bank on the existing home? (Reread the case studies to spark creative solutions for your unique situation.)

Be sure to include a reasonable timeframe for the real estate recovery and all of the costs to carry the property in the cost/benefit analysis. Don't forget mortgage payments are not your only expenses. So are insurance, maintenance, vacancies, remodels when a tenant leaves and property taxes. If you are paying money out of pocket on a place that will be underwater and illiquid for a decade or more, then you are back to square one – spending a lot of dough on something that is ruining your budget, your credit, your health, your life*style* and your life.

Bottom Line

Yes, it is *possible* that you will take a hit on your credit score if you short sale, foreclose or restructure your debt. However, if you are severely underwater on your mortgage or if the payments are bankrupting you and you are draining all of your assets to make payments, then it is more likely that your credit score will *improve* with a bankruptcy, foreclosure or short sale. If the asset is declining in value, the longer you hang on, the worse your cash bleed, assets to debt ratio and credit score become. Even if you give the home back or declare bankruptcy, you can keep your retirement plans, so tapping those accounts is a no-no. They are your lifeboat.

Take-Away Suggestions

1. You don't owe it to the bank to stay in a bad investment for two decades. Particularly when you consider that the bank's mortgage salesman was part of the team that likely lured you into the investment in the first place.

2. The real solutions to your situation lie in thinking outside the box. Use the cost-benefit analysis outlined in this chapter, rather than just trying to get the bank to

give you a loan modification (and relying on their decision as your only strategy).

3. Seek out the counsel of an accountant, a bankruptcy attorney and a family member whom you trust the judgment of. Run the cost-benefit analysis by them and factor in their recommendations to develop your best strategy.

Chapter 6: If You Are Underwater On Income Property

If you are underwater on income property, then you have to do a cost and benefit analysis on the investment, just like any business owner would. Because it is a business. Even if you are really attached to it.

Business Considerations for Income Property that is Underwater

1. Consider the marketplace.
2. Consider your costs to carry.
3. Consider when/if you can sell the investment for a profit.
4. Consider whether or not your money could be invested elsewhere for a superior return.
5. Factor in the costs of taxable "phantom" income. (These may be offset by your capital losses.)
6. Factor in the costs of borrowing at a higher interest rate, if you have to short sale, foreclose or do a deed in lieu.
7. Consider depreciation, business loss and capital losses.

In 2008, a couple came to me with a problem. A relative had convinced them to purchase a second home in 2006, right before real estate collapsed. This relative (who was getting a commission on the sale) convinced them that they were getting a great deal, even though they were losing more than $600 a month on the investment. (The renter was paying $600 less than their mortgage; their losses were greater if you factor in all of the other costs of owning property.) Additional costs of insurance (it was beach front in an earthquake prone city) and property taxes meant that this couple was spending at least $11,000 a year to keep the place, and that was on the prayer that no maintenance was needed. Meanwhile, the value of the home was dropping, which meant they couldn't re-finance or sell.

1. Consider the marketplace.

The statistics were dismal. In 2008, we were in the middle of a Great Recession. Unemployment was almost 10%. Foreclosures were at a record high and everyone knew someone who was getting foreclosed on. *At least* fifteen million people were in danger of losing their homes, according to my data analysis. (By the end of 2012, more than 12 million homes had entered the foreclosure process, with more to come in 2013, so my calculations in 2008 were on the money.)

All signs were that the market value of real estate in that area was going to continue to decline. The correction was predicted to be significant, and to continue at least through 2012. Since the average return of real estate is about 5%, I estimated that a decline of 25% in real estate could take six years to recover. If the conditions of the marketplace and my math turned out to be accurate, the couple would have to hold their property until 2017 before the value returned to their purchase price – at minimum. (In other areas of the U.S., the declines were 50% and more – meaning that you have to more than double the recovery time.)

2. Consider your costs to carry.

If my estimates were right (and they turned out to be spot on), then the couple would be flushing over $120,000 down the drain over an 11-year period, with little opportunity to sell the property or increase the rent. If they needed to replace a roof, or had mold issues (it was on the beach), or if there was an earthquake or fire, then their losses could be significantly higher. And if the renter moved out or didn't pay rent or became a problem, there was more exposure for losses as well.

3. Consider when/if you can sell the investment for a profit.

Once you add $110,000 in "costs to carry" to the property depreciation, and a five-year process of the bottoming out of real estate, they could be waiting another eight years to recover their investment. 14 years underwater is a long time. It's easy to see that this money could be better invested elsewhere, particularly since the partners were nearing 50 – at an age when they need to be squirreling away funds for retirement. In fact, because one of the partners was in the construction business, they would need to tap their retirement to keep the place – something that is almost always a no-no, particularly for people 50+.

4. **Consider whether or not your money could be invested elsewhere for a superior return.**

   $10,000 Year Invested + 10% Return

Year	Deposit	10% Gain*	Year End
1	$10,000	$1,000	$11,000
2	$10,000	$2,100	$23,100
3	$10,000	$3,310	$36,410
4	$10,000	$4,641	$51,051
5	$10,000	$6,105	$67,156
6	$10,000	$7,716	$84,872
7	$10,000	$9,487	$104,359
8	$10,000	$11,436	$125,795
9	$10,000	$13,579	$149,374
10	$10,000	$15,937	$175,311
11	$10,000	$20,384	$205,695
TOTAL	$110,000	$95,695	$205,695

10% annualized gain is completely doable. Both stocks and bonds have earned more than 10% annually over a 30-year period – including the Great Recession.

If $10,000 were invested and achieved a 10% gain each year, the couple would almost double their dough over the 11-year period. Instead of being negative $125,000 (or more), they would be positive $205,695.

5. Factor in the costs of taxable "phantom" income.

This couple came to me early in the game, so their phantom taxable income, since this was not their primary residence, would have still been rather small – particularly when compared to the losses they would endure over the next decade, if they did not negotiate to give the property back to the bank. It was so early in the Great Recession that they could have negotiated a Deed in Lieu, which is easier on your credit and creates no phantom income. (Many smart people in a similar position did this.) For others, even if the phantom income is large, the right answer might be to give the property back, restructure and move on. (It has been for other real estate investors, including Donald Trump.) You need professional help, however. An attorney should review the paperwork to make sure that the debt is discharged properly and not just sold to a debt collection agency. Your accountant will help to navigate the complicated tax reporting, considering phantom income (a 1099 event that is reported to the IRS), depreciation, capital loss, business loss, etc.

6. **Factor in the costs of borrowing at a higher interest rate.**

This couple already owned their own home and had a fixed rate on it. Their credit score before this fiasco was quite high. Even if they had to give the place back to the bank, in a foreclosure rather than a deed in lieu, their credit score should have been fully recovered by 2013 (within 5-7 years), as well – without impacting the interest rate on their primary residence. If they kept the property, their credit score would have gone down even if they made all of their payments on time, as their debt would increase, while their equity contracted. (The loan was an interest-only ARM loan that would was due to reset at a much higher rate in two years.)

7. **Consider depreciation, business loss and capital losses.**

In the case where you are severely underwater on your income property, there are many considerations. A business loss or a capital loss might completely offset any phantom income created by a bank forgiving some of the debt. You also have to factor in depreciation. If your losses make you insolvent, then business bankruptcy might allow you to restructure the debt, while still having a business that can make other investments going forward on better terms (think Trump Entertainment). That is why you really need to consult an experienced accountant and attorney before taking action. In the case study I've outlined here, this couple could have had a capital or business loss for their taxes, or no taxable phantom income, provided they acted soon enough. During real estate pullbacks, the longer you wait, the worse it gets.

Since the bank can resell the property, what *sounds* horrible – deed in lieu, foreclosure or short sale – is actually a win-win for everyone.

Are 10% Gains Achievable?

NASDAQ earned 75% gains between 2009 and 2011. At that pace (37.5% Annualized Return on Investment), the couple would have over $1 million at the end of eleven years, instead of *losing* $100,000 or more. They could purchase five homes in many parts of the United States with *cash*! (The average home price in October of 2012 was $183,900.)

Seek Professional Help

Before choosing deed in lieu, foreclosure, short sale or business or personal bankruptcy, you need to explore your rights with legal counsel and your tax ramifications (phantom income, etc.) with an accountant. You want to make sure that the shortfall isn't sold to a debt collector, that the taxes on phantom income don't bury you or that your income isn't levied. You cannot trust the bank or debt collector to look out for your best interests or even provide you with accurate information about all of the options available to you. That's simply not their job. A fair agreement needs to be spelled out in the contract and you need to clearly understand exactly what the terms of the contract are before signing it.

Bottom Line

Don't let the FICO Score Myth keep you swimming in the rip tide of compounding debt. Swimming sideways – finding a way to shore — is the best way to save yourself from drowning in debt. Trying to stay afloat will wear you out, slowly take you down, until eventually you drown.

Take-Away Suggestions

1. When evaluating how best to handle income property that is underwater, consider taxes, costs to carry, true market value, real returns on real estate, stocks and bonds, and whether the money could be better invested elsewhere for a superior return.
2. The sooner you do the math and seek out solutions, the easier it will be to extricate yourself from a bad situation and the sooner that you can focus your attention on income-producing passive investments.

3. Don't stick your head in the sand and fool yourself into thinking you don't have options, or that going along with the current plan will keep your credit rating high. Going from negative to positive requires sober thinking, a sound plan and thorough, professional execution from experts who are on your side (not on the debt collector's payroll).

Part 3: The Thrive Budget

Chapter 7: Don't Just Survive. Thrive!

Try my Thrive Budget, rather than your Buried Alive in Bills budget.

Are you thriving and loving your life, or are you just surviving from paycheck to paycheck and running out of money before the end of the month? Cutting out cafe lattes will not change anything in your life. Getting your big-ticket items in a reasonable range will launch you into dream come true living VERY FAST!

The Thrive Budget

My Thrive Budget™, upon which these rules are based, is outlined in greater detail in my book You Vs. Wall Street.

The Thrive Budget is based upon a simple formula that you should be limiting your basic needs expenditures to 50% of your budget, while the other half should be empowering you to thrive.

Here's the basic premise.

1. **Invest the first 10% of your income into a tax-protected retirement account.** This should be pre-tax

or tax deductible, such as a 401k, individual retirement account (IRA), health savings account (HSA), etc. If you aren't doing this, you are giving too much money to Uncle Sam.

2. **Donate 10% of your income to your favorite charity.** This is tax deductible.

3. **Invest 10% of your income on education.** This may be tax deductible. Ask your accountant. If you are well educated, then you'll be paying on this for a long time, however, you will also benefit from being very employable and earning a great income.

4. **Spend 20% of your income on fun and things that bring you pleasure.** This is probably not tax deductible, but it makes life worth living! Many times, having fun pre-allocated in your budget means that you'll actually be spending *less* and enjoying more. Fun offers free endorphins and anti-oxidants, which are also very good for your health.

5. **Limit all of your basic needs to just 50% of your income, including your home, insurance, car, food, clothes and taxes.**

10 Rules of Becoming Rich

Here are more details on how the Thrive Budget™ works.

1. Give yourself a raise.

10% of your net income should go on auto-deposit into your 401(k), IRA, health savings account, etc. First. Period. It's tax deductible. Pay yourself now, or pay the IRS later. If you invest right, your nest egg should earn 10% while you sleep, meaning your money will be worth more than your salary in seven years and will out-earn you in 25 years. People who start at 20 could be in a position to retire at 45. It's important to start early and be religious about this fiscally healthy habit.

2. Be charitable.

Tithe 10% to charity. Fuel your favorite cause with your cash, take the tax write-off and reap the benefits of helping your community and networking with others who have like-minded goals! You will find *your people* through your charity networks, so I recommend that you pick one that you can donate your time to, as well. The best, career moves I've ever made came directly from the relationships that I developed through my charitable giving. Pay your favorite charity now, or pay the IRS later.

3. Educate yourself, your family and others.

Education is the single highest correlating factor with income. Surgeons make more money than dishwashers, and surgeons who have educated themselves about investing make greater gains than those who invest blindly (or not at all). According to the Bureau of Labor Statistics, full-time workers without a high school diploma earned $451/week on average in 2011, compared to $1,053 for a Bachelor's Degree, and $1,551/week for professionals with a doctoral degree. PhDs, medical, business and law students often sleep on a couch (or small dorms) for years, in order to double or triple their income for life!

Limiting your expenses in order to educate yourself is something that can completely transform your life. A century ago, Asian immigrants were discriminated against and paid slave wages in the U.S. Today, Asians earn more money than any other ethnic group. A strong focus on education, and a willingness on the part of parents to sacrifice their own lifestyle for the sake of educating their children, shifted the economics for Asian Americans.

4. Have fun.

Health is wealth. You can't earn a great living if you can't get out of bed. And pleasure is a free endorphin that releases anti-oxidants that keep you healthy and sexy. What a beautiful reason to have some fun today!

The truth is that if you aren't setting aside money for fun, you are probably overspending and not even enjoying it. Shopaholics try retail therapy when they are unhappy, but it never works because the overriding mood in that scenario is one of desperation – not elation. In the Thrive Budget, you set aside time and money for fun no matter what and you spend it on things you enjoy. I take out 10% in cash, since fun is not tax deductible. That's more fun for me than counting receipts.

5. Double your pleasure.

Double your fun budget! Make sure that you are spending 20% of your income for FUN. You are worth it!

In truth, for a lot of people, this category is where you put that extra fun that you are not ready to give up in your "basic needs" category. For some people, it's spending a little more on their home – whether it is on a pool, a better neighborhood or just an extra room so the kids can each have one of their own. For others, it might be spending a little more on the car. Mine is often spent on a really adventurous vacation that I can enjoy with my family and friends. If you are going to spend your extra fun money on your home, car, etc., the next tip is a critical piece of the equation.

6. Stop complaining.

Some people say, "I spend my fun money on my home," and then, in the same breath, complain that they don't take vacations. That's clearly not fun. If you are going to spend your *fun* money on your home, then you have to start enjoying your home more. Can you have artist salons, or a front porch bayou Bluegrass party where someone blows on a jug and another plays spoons? A barbecue and three-legged race? A monthly yoga potluck dinner? Clearly, if you're complaining instead of having fun, then you can't put this in the fun category. And if your home is costing you an arm and a leg, then what kind of a way is that to go limping through life. Get creative about reducing your big-ticket items and you will find yourself with a lot more dough to thrive on – and a lot fewer reasons to complain.

7. Basic needs must be under 50%, including taxes.

Ha! Think this is impossible? Steve Jobs dropped out of college, slept on the floor of his friend's dorm room, walked to the Hari Krishna Temple for free meals, audited some of the classes he was most interested in, and then founded the most valuable company in the world. As of November 2012, Apple was worth half a trillion dollars. When immigrants are trying to get ahead, they focus on education. If two families have to live in a two-bedroom apartment so that the kids can go to medical school, they do that. I know a father of four who slept on his parent's couch while he attended graduate school. He became the CEO and chairman of a multi-billion dollar company. His kids are very happy now (although times were tough then).

As a single mother, I used house sharing to double the strength of my dollar. So did Gloria Allred, the famous women's advocate attorney. One of Neil Simon's funniest plays was based on two divorced men living together – *The Odd Couple.*

8. Think partner, not competitor.

Remember back in the 1970s when malls were created! By teaming up to put everything you need in one place, all of the retail stores benefitted. Coachella (and Woodstock before it) puts all of the greatest bands in one spot for an entire weekend. Crowds came.

Today, most people only have a piece of the equation when it comes to both income and passive income. If your credit is shot from bad real estate investments, but you have cash on hand, can you partner to buy income-producing real estate at a low-interest rate? If you have too much cash in savings, earning 0%, can you offer a trust deed to your kids, secured by their home, and earn a better rate of return?

No great achievement was ever created by one person acting alone. What can you do to partner up and create a win-win for everyone – particularly in this time of slow growth, high debt and bailed out banks?

9.   Dream bigger.

When John D. Rockefeller went into the oil business, in 1863, no one dreamed of freeways. When Google founders Sergey Brin and Larry Page began perfecting online search with results revealed in nanoseconds, most people were still on dial-up. When President John F. Kennedy promised to walk on the moon, it still took a week to mail a letter from New York to San Francisco. When John Lennon and Yoko Ono sang that the War Was Over, in 1971, the Vietnam War was still raging (but ended in 1975). What great dream do you have? What can you do now to start on the path of creating it and who can help you with it? As Larry Page, the co-founder and CEO of Google, says, "I think it is often easier to make progress on mega-ambitious dreams. I know that sounds completely nuts. But, since no one else is crazy enough to do it, you have little competition."

10. Health & Health Savings Accounts.

I first mentioned Health Savings Accounts in the debt section. If you are a healthy person and you are paying a lot of money for a low deductible health insurance policy, then you are making the insurance company rich. Get more details on IRS.gov. One trick I'll tell you is that you want to purchase your HSA from a brokerage rather than from the insurance company. That way you have control over what it is invested in. HSAs are tax deductible. The capital gains earned are not taxed. The money works as a retirement plan if you don't have to access the funds.

However, good health is just as important as saving money on your health insurance. Good health allows you to work, to enjoy life and to think clearly. So, when you are thinking of fun, education and even basic needs, be sure to include habits, strategies and fun that promote good health. Should you buy a gym membership? Would that be fun? Should you allocate a little more of your basic needs for organic food? Can you buy directly from farmers at a Farmers' Market?

21 days off the grid.

Stuck in a rut? Having a hard time embracing the Thrive Budget and a more sustainable lifestyle? 21 days is all you need to create new possibilities. If you have never been on a 21-day sabbatical, there is no greater way to expand your possibilities and your thinking. Whether it is an *Eat. Pray. Love* journey, or an ashram experience, or a trek to Mt. Everest, or a road trip to see family, or a love jaunt to the Cote d'Azur or training to be the first rock star to perform on the moon, commit to creating something new and exciting in your life. And if you cannot take time off from work, then find a new, good habit that you want to embrace and commit to living, breathing and thinking about it for a full 21 days. After 21 days, it will become your new reality and good habit.

Why is 21 days off the grid and out of your routine so important? Your lizard brain fears change. Your passions love pleasure and adventure. So, when you fuel change with endorphins, you can think outside the box more easily, and whatever change you are trying to forge will be more permanent because you will associate that change with a fond memory. Many years ago, when I wanted to quit smoking, I kissed my boyfriend every time I wanted to have a cigarette. It worked much better than a nicotine patch.

Creative thinking is often just what is needed when you have had blind faith in something that has created a living hell for you. Guilt and remorse shut down thinking. They are by definition a focus on the past – what has already happened. The key is to focus on the future, to think about new possibilities, to commit to a pathway and to walk forward and diligently to achieve your dreams.

Yes, visualizing that beautiful tomorrow is a piece of the puzzle. But if you don't set out and walk forward, you'll never arrive. As Lao Tzu says, "The journey of a thousand miles begins with a single step."

Bottom Line

Dreaming without a plan is just a wish. Guilt and remorse are simply sitting in the mud puddle, whining to the passersby about how filthy you are. Chances are many have been in the same position. They just got up, showered off and are not defined by that event. So, sing your song… loudly. Dance as if everyone is watching. (They are … on your social networks…) And fall in love with your ability to transform your smart Thrive Budget™ into the power that fuels your dream come true life.

Success story to be inspired by

One of the richest women in the world, J.K. Rowling, received public assistance while she created one of the most beloved stories of all time – Harry Potter.

Take-Away Suggestions

1. Take a 21-day vacation from the status quo. Try the Eternal City (Rome) or Paris or Machu Picchu or the hometown you haven't seen in forever. You could use it.
2. Dream bigger. Not everyone writes a bestselling book or stars in an Academy-Award winning film. But everyone does have something unique to give to the world.
3. 50% to survive and 50% to Thrive!

Chapter 8: Shopping for Success – Literally.

Should you buy an expensive house or car or invest in your wardrobe to increase your income?

Investing in a Neighborhood

Buying a home in the right neighborhood can pay off in many, many ways. The public schools might be better. You might meet successful people while walking the dog. Your children play sports with the children of people who value education, investing, income and passive income and will grow up "understanding" money. So, this can in fact be an excellent investment. If you buy at a reasonable price (real estate prices in 2012 were at a decade low, on average), and if you finance at a reasonable rate (interest rates were at an all-time low at the end of 2012), then you have a great neighborhood to live in, an excellent tax deduction (in the U.S.) and the chance that the value of your home will increase in value in the coming years.

As I discuss in greater detail in the "hard assets" chapter, hard assets will perform better than paper assets going forward. So, it's better to move some nest egg money into a great home than to have all of your dough sitting in your 401K or IRA or annuity or retirement plan. That is even more pronounced if a large portion of your nest egg is invested in the company that you work for. While no one wants to think that their company could experience hardship, United Airlines pilots, Enron employees and GM workers have all experienced losses in their retirement plans. ARISA guidelines are that no more than 10% of your nest egg should be in the company you work for. You should be diversifying your nest egg into funds – and not in *any* individual company at all. Stocks on steroids (individual companies) are high risk and high maintenance. You have to babysit them. Funds have the benefit of having a lot of companies, so that if one does poorly, another can do well.

Leveraging your nest egg money is one way to get into a better neighborhood than you could otherwise. Your home can definitely be a piece of that 10% "pay yourself first" investing money, from the Thrive Budget. It should not be 100% of your investments because a home is illiquid. If you need the money, it can take months to access (through a home equity line of credit), and if you need a lot of money, it could take months or years to sell the property. So, put some of your income into a tax-protected retirement account, too.

Since the neighborhood you live in might keep you from having to pay private school tuition for your kids, you can also have a piece of your education budget going to your home. And if you really love the neighborhood, then it can also be fun.

As you can see from this, what the Thrive Budget is intended to do is to align your expectation with a reasonable return. It is reasonable that a home in a good neighborhood will equal a better education, particularly if you have researched the schools. It is reasonable that it will be more fun, unless you are a vacation junkie who will be deprived of adventure. It is definitely a good idea to start moving paper assets into hard assets, particularly if you can buy at a 10-year low and finance at interest rates of 4% or lower! That's almost free money! As we discussed in the real estate case studies, even if you think you don't have a down payment, or good credit, you may be able to partner with someone who does. The most important consideration, where most people get it wrong, is: "Can you really afford the home, based upon the allocations of the Thrive Budget?"

Investing in a Car

Car lovers will try to convince themselves that a fancy car will bring them more income because it impresses people. The truth is that successful people know how to spot a poor person who is leasing an expensive car.

Having said that, because people are in such financial straits right now, I've seen Ferraris, and other classic cars, liquidated on the cheap. The trick would be having a good mechanic, a good understanding of the marketplace and an inside track into a seller who is too desperate (or discrete) to auction it off.

As with any investment, you must factor in the costs to carry the investment, when you are considering what your return on investment might be. You must factor in insurance, wear and tear, accidents, theft, etc. If the investment is intended to impress people, in order to increase your income (and that is the rationale that you are using to "make the investment") remember that cars only impress naïve people – not successful people. A good investment is a leader in the sector that you purchase at a great price and has the opportunity to be sold later at an even better price.

There is one other type of car that I want you to consider, an electric vehicle. With the costs of gasoline in 2012, the savings of having an electric vehicle, particularly if you can use solar power to juice it up, make this investment very attractive. The payback, considering your gas savings, can be just a few years and shorter if you consider the tax incentives. Tax laws change every year, so be sure to consult with an accountant and/or research on IRS.gov before assuming that there will be a tax break on your EV purchase.

Could you ride a bike or take public transportation to work? Biking to work promotes fiscal and physical health (providing the roads are safe) and definitely goes a long way to beautifying your bottom line.

Investing in Charity

When I donate to charity, I consider it an investment in making the world a better place. Every cent you own and every moment you spend is always an investment, so 10% of my time and money are invested in making the world a better place – which means my world is a better place, too. You'll find that the people you meet who are also doing that will have a lot of other interests in common with you, and are genuinely interested in you and your success. Start by donating your time and talent, if you feel you don't have money to give yet. If you are a parent, this sets a great example for your kids, which pays off for life. Most people don't consider charity to be a part of their Shopping for Success Plan, but if you focus your time, talent and money, sit on the board, become a part of the decision-making, etc., you'll see that it does indeed increase your own personal success as well because you become a respected individual in the community.

Investing in a Wardrobe

Every job, promotion and raise I ever got hinged on one critical heel—dressing the part. Have you ever heard of anyone in a t-shirt and thongs (the shoes, not the underwear) getting an executive level position (unless they owned the company)? How would you feel if your attorney showed up to court in a Hawaiian shirt or your gardener came to work in a tuxedo?

Every job has its standard dress code, and dressing for success is a subtle, but important statement that you *belong there.* And that message has to start *before* you ask for the job, not after. Unfortunately, you *can't afford* to rationalize that you'll buy the new suit after you get the job and have the extra money to afford it. If you don't invest in the duds first, your big shot will be a blank.

The reason that I say to start walking the talk now, is that it's not just in the boss' office where that suit can be an advantage. Great-looking clothes (and every fashionista knows that fabric DOES matter) can provide a conversation starter for strangers. I met one of my business advisors at a conference because he and I were standing in the valet queue, waiting for our respective cars, wearing similar his and her pin-stripe suits, crafted by the same designer. (Yes, I bought mine at a marked discount, on sale, which is something anyone can do easily in 2012.) That suit sparked a business relationship and Rolodex sharing that launched my company.

Still afraid to pony up the dough before you win the job? Worried about how you'll pay off the credit card bill? Unfortunately, it's a Catch 22 situation. If you don't make the investment, you're unlikely to get the job. However, you don't always have to pay retail, and sometimes you don't have to spend anything at all, to get what you need. Is there a great resale shop close by? Do you have an aunt or uncle who dresses well and might hand you down something? Have you looked into a nonprofit organization that specializes in business attire?

When you are looking for a raise and promotion, which strategy is more likely to succeed? Walking into your boss' office wearing what you always wear or having the boss walk by your desk and see you looking sharp and brand spanking new, like s/he'd better promote you before one of her clients snatches you up?

Last week, I came across an executive assistant wearing a tailored suit. The first thing I thought was, "Wow! If her work ethic, her education and her intelligence warrant a raise and promotion, I wouldn't be surprised to see her in her own office next time I visit." (And if her education and industry acumen don't measure up, then her next shopping spree should be for college classes and/or professional development!) I put her name on my short list of people I would approach when my company hires.

Before you trip on over to the designer outlet mall, measure up your education. If you've been hitting your head on the glass ceiling for a while, make sure that you've got the degree you need for the job. Odds are against you getting a great job without the right education and credentials, no matter what you're wearing.

So take a moment to envision that dream-come-true job and you dancing in those 'to-die-for' shoes. Be willing to invest in your education and an appropriate wardrobe, to jump a rung or two up the ladder! Do not succumb to shopaholic behavior, however. That bad habit usually ends back up at the dead-end of struggling to survive because you are buried alive in bills.

And if you're really happy where you are, don't sweat it. Climbing the corporate ladder has no bearing on what kind of person you are anyway. In his book, *Giving*, President Clinton describes a laundress who saved up a quarter of a million dollars for charity. What a rich life she led! Just be the best *you*, and know that living the life of your dreams can be created no matter what you are wearing.

Finally, get the most bang for your buck. The New Year can be a great time for sales. Paying a little more for a great fabric and a great cut can pay off for years because classic designs don't go out of fashion, like the latest trend does. Off-the-rack suits and outrageous fashion statements may cost less, but they also look cheaper and wear out in just one season. Whereas a great suit can become this year's hip, new look with a new hemline, blouse and some accessories!

Bottom Line

Shopping for success is very different than "keeping up with the Joneses" or retail therapy. By being mindful about the price you pay, the return you expect and how that fits into your Thrive Budget, you can achieve exactly what you most desire.

Take-Away Suggestions

1. A comfortable home that you purchase for an affordable price, in a good neighborhood, at an all-time low mortgage rate, is a great investment for many reasons.

2. Hard assets will perform better than paper assets (including "money") in the years to come. Take a serious look at your paper money (annuity, 401K, pension, IRA, savings) and see how that might be better put to work.

3. Shopping for success can work if you are spending on assets that really have a chance to pay off in terms of income or passive income. Retail therapy usually just creates debt and unhappiness.

Chapter 9: Grade Your Guru Before You Buy Into Anything.

The "free lunch" seminar could give you far more problems than indigestion.

I originally wrote this chapter one day after the world was supposed to end. Harold Camping, the president of Family Radio (based out of California), predicted that the world would end on May 21, 2011, beginning at 6:00 p.m. in your time zone. He's still not sure how he got it wrong. It's a bit perplexing, however, this wasn't the first time Camping got the date of the Apocalypse wrong. He tried to whirl up a frenzy back in 1994 as well.

Another guru with failed predictions predicted *The Roaring 2000s* – that the Dow Jones Industrial Average would hit "at least 21,500 and likely higher." He predicted "the greatest boom in history" six months before the NASDAQ began its slide down a canyon of losses totaling 75%. NASDAQ bottomed out at a low of 1,114 on October 9, 2002, and, since then, has come only a little more than half of the distance of the high of 5060, set on March 10, 2000. The Dow Jones Industrial

Average spent most of the last decade below 11,000, and bottomed out at 6547 on March 9, 2009.

At that point, rather than admit defeat, the same author had a new prophecy – that America was in a Great Depression. This book was released at the end of 2009 (almost a year after the lowest point in the markets). Over the next three years, NASDAQ more than doubled and the Dow Jones Industrial Average enjoyed gains of 50+%.

Investors that followed this author's suggestion of moving into the euro to protect themselves, would have bankrupted themselves. Funds like MF Global, with too much exposure to Greek bonds, went belly-up. The other suggestions of bonds and Treasury bills were earning dismal, or negative, returns, instead of rolling in the returns of stocks. Though bonds performed well in the years prior to 2009, they stalled out in the aftermath, worldwide, due to excessive debt in almost all of the developed world and many corporations.

Whether it is a doomsday prophet or a cheerleader tossing out the sure-fire fix with his data or the person you hired to "manage your money," your first move isn't to listen and believe everything they tell you. It is to grade the guru, to determine if s/he is worthy of listening to at all. Especially if the guru is on a stage, even more so if you were offered free lunch, and critically important if they have control over your nest egg and future.

One of my subscribers asked me about a guru who had already been convicted of being a scam artist! The scam artist was speaking on the stage of a bestselling author, so the listener assumed he was legitimate. However, a simple Internet search revealed this "expert" had a history of problems with the Securities and Exchange Commission. A few years prior, subscribers paid over a million to him, when he promised them that he would "DOUBLE YOUR MONEY ON MAY 22ND ON THIS SUPER INSIDER TIP." The e-mail was promoting a company that was involved in the nuclear energy field and was supposed to benefit from the arms reduction treaty between the U.S. and Russia.

Although this "expert" claimed that people made a lot of money by listening to his warnings and using his strategies, without providing testimonials or real proof of those happy campers, the strategies listed on his website would have *lost* a lot of money for people. If you began shorting stocks in December of 2008, as the guru advised, you would have lost a lot of dough because 2009 was an *outstanding* year on Wall Street. NASDAQ earned 40% – more than gold! The Dow Jones Industrial Average earned 15%. Shorting would have lost beaucoup money during that rally.

Are you surprised that, even after all of the hoopla on gold, NASDAQ beat gold in returns in 2009? And, believe it or not, NASDAQ is *far less risky* than gold is! The trouble with gold is that when it's hot, it's hot, and when it's not it's the worst performing asset, usually stagnating at returns that are lower than inflation. I'll discuss this more in the gold chapter. Between 2002 and 2011, gold earned 18% annually (taking my 2009 Company of the Year, U.S. Gold to a 19X return on investment!) Over the 30-year period, gold was less than 5% annualized gain. Meanwhile, small cap stocks earned 11.5% annually over 30 years.

When I see fear mongering (so common these days) with very little evidence to back it up, I start smelling a rat. There are definitely issues in the U.S.; however, the issues are worldwide, not limited to US alone. Many other countries are in far worse shape. PIIGS comes to mind – Portugal, Ireland, Italy, Greece and Spain. And those countries that are *perceived* to be in better shape (like say, China and Canada) are tied to the success of our future. We are the biggest customer of both countries.

The U.S. invents a lot of things that the rest of the world loves. We live in the most free country on the planet. We have oceans bordering the east and west of our continent, and two friendly, free neighbors to the north and south of us. By contrast, China is the most polluted nation on the planet and has to import our innovations (Google, Apple, etc.). China loves our products so much that many clean energy and technology companies rack up to 80% of their sales from Asia.

As Chinese President Hu said in his visit to the White House on January 21, 2011, "We [are] in the same boat and we should row in the same direction when we ... tackle challenges."

I am touting the strengths of the U.S. but that doesn't mean I'm a Pollyanna all of the time. I did in fact predict the bankruptcy of General Motors, the stock crashes of Freddie Mac and Fannie Mae and the Great Recession. GM's troubles were outlined specifically in my book, *You Vs. Wall Street*, which I penned in 2006 – three years before GM's bankruptcy. My Great Recession prediction in January of 2008 and simple way to get safe, which was published in my ezine and also distributed through an email alert, *made money* during the Great Recession. And I started my business with a warning to investors to get out of Fannie Mae and Freddie Mac – as early as 2003.

All of my research is available online 24/7, dating back to 2003. I have many testimonials from happy investors who have incorporated my strategies in bull and bear markets quite successfully more than 12 years. Perhaps the biggest testimonials I have are TD AMERITRADE chairman Joe Moglia and Nobel Prize winning economist Dr. Gary Becker, who penned the Preface to *You Vs. Wall Street*, writing, ""Many people, including educated men and women, get into trouble when they neglect to follow the simple rules in this book. That is why I recommend it with enthusiasm."

You might think it is tough to distinguish between the testimonials of Moglia and Becker and a bestselling author who hosts a "guru" on his stage. But it isn't really as tough as you think. If someone is on the stage of a bestselling author, you can bet that person is paying the author to be on that stage, or giving him/her a commission on any sales. You can't buy the testimonial of the TD AMERITRADE chairman or the University of Chicago professor (Dr. Becker). As is the case in all things dealing with salesmen, you should follow the money (i.e. know how much they are receiving to "endorse" whatever it is that they are selling) and do a thorough background check, paying particular attention to fines, jail time, law suits, complaints and investigations.

Is your financial planner employed by one of the brokerages that was fined by the SEC and/or bailed out? Factor that into the equation when you listen to the recommendations. Know what a healthy portfolio looks like, so that you can spot any discrepancies. And use the questions outlined in the "Brokers are Salesmen," chapter of *You Vs. Wall Street* to understand the qualifications of your financial team. Before you hand the reins of your future to anyone, interview them as if your life depended upon it because your life*style* does.

If your guru has been in business for longer than seven years, with no complaints and no problems with regulators, that's a good start, but it is not the only consideration. Today's world is very different from the buy and hold world of yesteryear. The most experienced money managers need to keep up with the times, just as a surgeon would need to learn laser surgery, rather than rely on the old school slice and dice. In fact, one of the best places for quality, timely information on stocks and bonds is FINRA.org, the financial industry regulatory authority. You can also check up on the track record of any financial professional there.

Having an Ivy League MBA or a big job sounds impressive, but that doesn't mean anything either, unfortunately. The author I outlined at the beginning of this chapter has a Harvard MBA. Bernie Madoff was the non-executive chairman of the NASDAQ stock market. Dr. Myron Scholes won a Nobel Prize for writing his options theory, and yet his hedge fund Long-Term Capital Management went bankrupt. Secretary of the Treasury Henry Paulson, who oversaw the biggest bailout in the history of the United States, was the chairman and CEO of Goldman Sachs when all of the derivative troubles were reaching their zenith.

Bottom Line

A great guru will have a PhD in *results*, and you'll be able to see those results easily when you request them. Results, over the last ten years, are more valuable than any Ivy League MBA. So, grade your guru by how well her strategies have worked before you waste any time learning from her. One or two years of outstanding gains hasn't stood the test of time, and dismal 10-year performance from a former superstar indicates an outdated strategy. Avoid the free lunch. Invest your education dollars wisely. One could cost you an arm and a leg. The other could buy you financial freedom for life.

Take-Away Suggestions

1. Use your education money to increase your skill set for income and passive income. Avoid the "free lunch" seminars.
2. Don't buy into the panacea offered by snake-oil salesmen, who try to scare the living daylights out of you.
3. Trust results! Not a big name, a big job, a big title, an Ivy-League degree, a big stage or a slick sales pitch.

Part 4: Stocks

Chapter 10: The ABCs of Investing in a Debt World

Buy and Hold Doesn't Work.

Buy and hold hasn't worked for the last ten years and will not work going forward. Why? Because the U.S. is in a slow growth cycle – as are most developed countries that have low fertility rates and a large cohort entering retirement. Pile on a $16 trillion debt and a partisan political system that is "kicking the can" of necessary tax and entitlement reform down the road, and you've got years of drag on GDP growth. And yet, amid that dreary future, there will continue to be boom and bust cycles, fueled by free, easy Fed money, ambitious, creative entrepreneurs and high-frequency traders. (The Feds are predicting low interest rates through mid-2015.)

NASDAQ and the Dow are Still Underwater

Twelve years ago, NASDAQ was above 5000. Five years ago, the Dow Jones Industrial Average hit an all-time high of 14,164. As of November 15, 2012, NASDAQ is still only worth a little more than half of its all-time high, at 2836. The Dow

Jones Industrial Average dropped all the way down to 6547 in March of 2009, and, after four years, has still not crawled its way back to even. The other problem with the Buy and Hold strategy today is that each time you lose half, your nest egg takes twice as long to recover. A 10% gain on $100,000 is $10,000, but a 10% gain on $50,000 is only $5,000. So, even if the markets resurface, your nest egg is still underwater.

On the other hand, our Federal Reserve and Treasury Department are able to fuel economic growth with cheap, easy money (if you can access it). That means that there has been and will continue to be boom and bust cycles. The good news about 0% interest rates is the opportunities that creates for investors, corporations and businesses. The bad news is that if you are not rebalancing your nest egg at least once a year, your phenomenal gains can evaporate and take years (if not decades) to return. And if you purchased your property at the top of the market, then you might be trapped in a home that is worth a lot less than your low-interest mortgage – costing you an arm and a leg, as well as your credit rating.

NASDAQ doubled between 1998 and 2000, and then imploded, giving up 75% from 2000-2002. Gold has been hot for the last decade, but if you bought at $1,895, you've been underwater for over a year. (And, it's important to remember that if you purchased gold at the high in 1980, you had to wait 29 years for the value of your investment to return.) Clean energy was the top industry in 2007, with almost 60% gains, and has been the worst performer ever since – from 2008-2012. Bonds were on fire 2001-2002, but legacy corporations (auto and airline industries) have defaulted since that time, making credit risk a big concern. Municipalities and sovereign nations have been downgraded. Credit risk, in places never before imagined, abounds.

What do you do in this environment? You must know the ABCs of Investing in a Debt World, where many developed nations and large corporations are carrying substantial – unsustainably high – debt loads. The strategies of *The ABCs of Money* were first presented in *You Vs. Wall Street* and have been featured in my Investor Educational Retreats over the last decade. In the *results* test, these strategies have worked fantastically for more than a decade now, through bull and bear markets, at a time when almost every other system has failed. (That is why readers have called *You Vs. Wall Street* a must-read financial bible.)

As Linda wrote to me last year when the U.S. credit was downgraded for the first time in history, "With all that is going on... because I follow Natalie's Thrive Budget Model, I am calm through this wild time and doing a little 'shopping' everyday for stocks that were on my list and reached a price I was waiting for!"

You Vs. Wall Street offers a lot of strategies for picking winning companies and individual stocks, and some basics on budgeting and nest egg strategies. However, the world has changed so dramatically – that book was penned in 2007 – that I knew it was time to go into far greater detail now. The annual and seasonal Wall Street trends changed dramatically. Bonds used to be an easy way to get safe, but, with the significant credit risk in the Debt World, bonds can be one of the most vulnerable assets to hold!

The ABCs of Investing in a Debt World.

1. Pay Yourself First (Not the Bill Collectors).

Putting 10% of your income into a 401k, IRA, Health Savings Account or other tax-protected retirement account – religiously – provides both offense and defense. You can score gains and your money can compound. Plus it is protected from any financial predator, including lawsuits, debt collectors, lien holders and banks. As I wrote earlier, when your gains compound, you can become financially free. When your debt compounds, you are enslaved by your bills. Do not wait until you get out of debt to start saving and investing. You will never get out of debt and become financially free, if you do not score gains and assets (income and passive income) – starting here and now.

According to the IRS, "Generally, amounts in your IRA (including earnings and gains) are not taxed until distributed. In some cases, amounts are not taxed at all if distributed according to the rules." So, put 10% of your income into a tax-protected retirement account, so that it receives favorable tax treatment and is safe from financial predators, including you dipping your hand in the jar when you want a new toy.

2. Hard Assets vs. Paper Assets.

In a world of credit risk and inflation, safe, cash-positive, income-producing hard assets are desirable. Your paper money will buy less in the inflationary years to come, whereas your home, income property or even classic car could become more valuable. Always buy at a great price – which is entirely possible today when most things are on fire sale. Financing terms at the end of 2012 were at a historic low. I'll discuss how to evaluate hard assets in that section of *The ABCs of Money*.

3. What's Safe?

Don't overreach your budget and capital potential. Understand the carrying costs of any investment and do a sober analysis of the credit risk, interest rate risk, capital risk, natural disaster risk, global warming risk and default risk. Read the fine print of any document, including those from banks and credit card companies, and particularly with regard to annuities, high-yield CD products, etc. FDIC-insured is key for any paper assets that you have. Don't take on substantial risk for a few extra points in yield. Make sure that you understand each of the scenarios outlined in the fine print *clearly*. With regard to annuities, these are not FDIC-insured and they are definitely not as "safe" as you've been led to believe. If AIG had not been bailed out, American investors were at risk of losing tens of millions of annuities, valued in the trillions. The state guaranty funds could not have handled the load.

4. Stocks: Modern Portfolio Theory

Always keep a percentage equal to your age safe. Diversify the remaining funds by size and style. Add in hot industries. Avoid the Bailouts. Rebalance 1-3 times a year. Overweight safe in troubled times and/or if you are a Nervous Nelly. Continue reading this section for a detailed discussion on this, and sample pie charts of what this looks like.

5. Bonds: Credit Risk & Interest Rate Risk

Bondholders have thought they were safe because interest rates are at rock bottom and the Federal Reserve Board keeps promising to keep rates at rock bottom – through mid-2015 (as of November 16, 2012). However, credit risk is determining the interest rates of bonds – not interest rate risk. (The European Central Bank has interest rates at rock bottom, too, but that hasn't helped Greece to borrow money below 20% interest rates.) Credit risk is heightened today, as are defaults and downgrades. Learn how to evaluate debt and credit risk in the What's Safe section of this book.

6. Treasury Bills.

The good news is that the U.S. can print its own money. The bad news is that when that happens, the value of your dollar decreases. It's not likely that the U.S. will go out of business. It is likely that it will cost more to buy less in the years to come. If you buy T-bills, keep your terms short.

7. Foreign Currency.

The world is very interconnected, and there are a lot of flashy salesmen trying to earn commissions on your fear. The truth is that investing in currencies is a risky business that many *pros* avoid. Additionally, software sites that boast of 88% accurayc (with the word misspelled) aren't telling you that less than 2% of those using the software are actually make money. I've never known any high-octane trader who has earned consistent gains over more than a 2-year period. I know a lot who have gone belly-up. As for gold as a currency, fuel, food and water will be more popular on the bartering table in the Apocalypse.

8. **Real Estate.**

It's hard to get a loan today. Credit standards are high. However, with the lowest interest rates the world has ever known and real estate prices in the U.S. that are back to what they were a decade ago, real estate could be a great investment. You must do a sober analysis, however. Read the chapter on "Income Property". Remember that the average annualized gain of real estate is less than 5%. Many (but not all) U.S. cities have real estate that is much cheaper to buy than it is to rent. People with a lousy credit score have to rent, which puts income property owners in a great seat to buy and rent property — provided they find a good deal and good tenants. Yes, you might need a partner, so check out the possibilities in the Hard Assets section of *The ABCs of Money*.

In terms of just investing in REITs (Real Estate Investment Trusts that are publicly traded), however, you must be very careful. If the company went through the Great Recession, they probably have too much debt and are in the same position as homeowners who financed at the top of the market are. And if it is a non-public REIT, there are even more risks. In fact, FINRA.org has issued an Investor Alert on non-publicly traded REITs, which I encourage you to read.

9. **International Investing.**

This can add diversification to your nest egg and could also be a way of adding in hot industries. However, there are risks. For instance, in some countries, the election of a new President creates the risk that corporations will be nationalized. Know the risks, balance the amount of exposure that you take on and make sure that this hot industry is only a slice of your nest egg, not the whole pie. At my Investor Educational Retreats, we go into greater detail on how to analyze your funds, including international funds. So, if this is of great interest to you, then go to NataliePace.com and register to attend our next retreat.

10. **Annual Rebalancing.**

Rebalancing your nest egg at least once a year is critically important. If you were doing this, you would have captured your gains at the high in NASDAQ in 2000. You would have made money in real estate in 2005. You would have doubled your money on Australia and Latin America funds in 2009 (which were some of my hot picks). And you would have made money in the Great Recession, like Bill and Nilo Bolden did, instead of losing half, like most Americans.

Bottom Line

Buy and Hold strategies don't work on the Wall Street rollercoaster of the New Millennium. Modern Portfolio Theory, combined with a few other key strategies, does. Bonds are more vulnerable in today's world than you know, so start considering safe, hard assets – "things" like income property –

to position yourself best in a Debt World. You will still need some liquidity in the form of paper assets. And just because I'm underweight on bonds, in general, right now, doesn't mean that there are not opportunities to make money by investing in some high-quality offerings. (So be sure to read the What's Safe and Hard Assets sections.) Would you buy a Google or Apple bond, if you knew these companies had no debt, double-digit sales growth and tens of billions of cash?

Take-Away Suggestions

1. Income-producing hard assets, that you purchase at a great price, will perform better than most paper assets, including bonds, in the years to come.
2. Bonds, annuities and other "guaranteed" or "safe" assets are more vulnerable than you know.
3. Get educated on how to avoid the Bailouts and add in hot industries. Remember: the higher the yield, the higher the risk.

Chapter 11: Easy as a Pie Chart Investing

My simple 6-step easy-as-a-pie chart nest egg plan, which is based upon Modern Portfolio Theory, is far less complicated and time consuming than the plan you currently use. Even if you are ignoring your retirement plan, and filing the paperwork without looking at it, you know that worrying about money is keeping you up at night. It's very likely that not knowing what you are doing has cost you an arm and a leg in the past. On the other hand, once you set your budget and investing up right, you simply revisit the plan once a year. It's really that easy!

My pie chart strategies work whether Wall Street is exuberant or apocalyptic, mainly because you:

1) Have the right amount protected,

2) Avoid the Bailouts,

3) Are invested in hot industries and

4) Rebalance at least once a year to capture your gains and get enough safe.

I repeat. Overweighting safe, during the Bank Bailout Market Bust of 2008 and 2009 (known more commonly as the Great Recession), and, before that, the DOT COM Bust of

2000-2002, was the single-most efficacious tool for preserving your nest egg. (By the way, having a strong, easy plan that can be overweighted a little more safe, is not jumping in and out or market timing.) By overweighting safe, you could have limited your losses on the stock side to under 11% during the Great Recession, if you were over 50. Meanwhile, the bond side would have earned gains, meaning you might not have lost anything at all, or even earned money, while those around you lost so much. Bonds were the top-performing assets during the bear market of 2002, with gains of up to 25%! (Bonds are riskier today, so keep reading.)

6 Tips for Superior Nest Egg Performance

1. Always keep a percentage equal to your age safe.
2. Overweight safe in troubled times (or if you are a Nervous Nelly).
3. Know what is safe.
4. Diversify the remaining "at risk" portion of your liquid portfolio into 10 funds – small, medium, large, value and growth and 4 hot industries.
5. Avoid the Bailouts and industries with high debt.
6. Rebalance at least once a year.

Here are what the pie charts look like for a 25 and 50-year old.

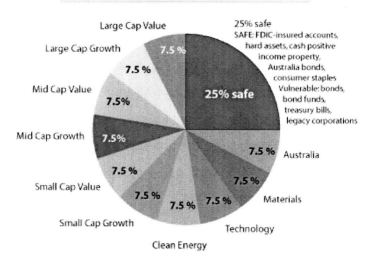

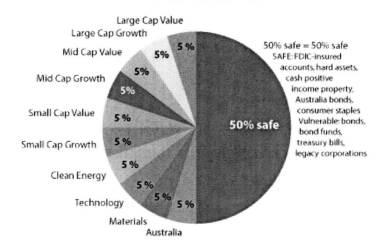

Here are what the pie charts with 20% overweighted safe look like.

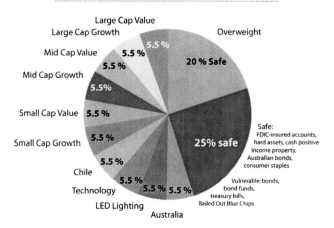

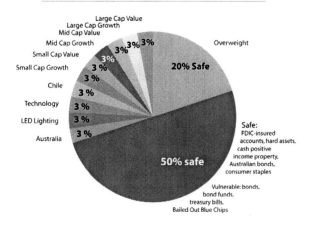

The reason that I list all six tips above, instead of just focusing on fund evaluation, is that the system itself helps you to pick the best funds. Also, it is even more important to be properly protected and diversified and to have a rebalancing strategy (to capture gains) than it is to get too crazy about picking the individual funds. During troubled times, it is your *safe* side that earns gains. *All* of the stock funds are vulnerable.

Performance of the Vanguard Total Bond Market Index Fund (VBMFX)

Compared to the Dow Jones Industrial Average and the NASDAQ Composite Oct. 1, 2007-April 1, 2009

Source: Money.MSN.com. Used with permission from Microsoft.

For most people, fund evaluation is going to involve figuring out how to reduce the pages and pages of funds and individual companies they currently own into 10 funds, diversified by size, style and sizzle (hot industries). For those of you who want to "evaluate" the funds themselves, remember that the actual holdings of the funds change, so it's not a great idea to buy a fund simply because you like one of the companies in it.

Since we've had a market recovery over the past few years, by the end of 2012 the only industries left behind in the value funds were the bailouts and companies with a lot of debt. This makes it more difficult to find good value funds. During market corrections, you can purchase value funds that include some high growth stocks, and in that scenario, the value fund should beat the growth fund in gains. At my Investor Educational Retreat, I teach creative ways to remain diversified without compromising the 6 Tips, and how to buy *all* of your funds at a good value. (If you don't know the difference between value and growth, or any other term used in this book, consult a good financial dictionary.)

There are literally tons of articles designed to help you select funds, and each one of the articles will reflect the overall philosophy of the company that is hosting the article (in the same way that a politician will shave the facts to support his position). The most important thing to superior nest egg performance is that you are able to employ all six steps listed above. If the fund terms prevent you from selling the fund without a penalty, that means you won't be able to rebalance and capture profits. If the fund has a lot of banks that were bailed out, or is heavy in industries that are carrying a lot of debt (like real estate), then superior performance requires a different industry makeup.

Here are More Details to Help You Set Up Your Nest Egg

1. **Add up the total value of all of your "nest eggs"** – i.e. your 401Ks (old & new), your IRA, your annuity and your savings. This total is what you want to consider as your nest egg pie chart. (Don't include real estate, your car, jewelry, or any other valuable collectible. Hard assets are part of your total asset value, but are non-liquid assets, whereas your nest egg deals with liquid, paper assets.)

2. **Keep a percentage equal to your age "safe."** As an example, if you have $100,000 in your 401K, IRA and savings account, and you are 50, you would be keeping $50,000 "safe." There are many assets that are safer than stock. Most of the time, you can overweight safe easily, using bonds, Treasury Bills, Certificates of Deposit and

FDIC insured savings accounts. These days, you have to be a lot more careful about bonds, even those that are highly rated. As I've said a lot in this book, safe, cash-positive, yielding hard assets – like income property – will do better in the years to come than paper assets. Read the fine print on all of your "safe" paper assets to be sure that they are as safe as you think. Is your high-yield certificate of deposit FDIC-insured? What kind of safety net does your annuity offer, if the insurance company gets into trouble, like AIG did? Is there any circumstance where the payback on your annuity, bond or fund might be less than you are counting on? Are you more at risk than you know? Ask the hard questions now, rather than being a dollar short at the end of the day, when you need it most. It is very important that your "safe" money is not at risk of loss of principal.

3. **Protect an additional 10-20% percent during recessions** and times of grave uncertainty. This is what I call overweighting safe.

4. **Take the remaining "pie" and divide that into ten slices.** One fund represents one "slice." Ten funds are easy to manage and easy to do the math on. Dozens of funds are confusing, hard to add up and thus, it is difficult to see your return on investment.

5. **Diversify six of the slices by size and style.** Small cap growth, small cap value, mid cap growth, mid cap value, large cap growth and large cap value. Why? Because different parts of the market perform differently. NASDAQ doubled off of its low in March 2009, whereas the Dow Jones Industrial Average recovered at half the speed. Small cap stocks returned 7.05% annually between 2002 and 2011, while the large companies made only 2.9% annually over the same period. In general, small caps add performance and large caps add stability. Value means you are buying the company stock on sale and growth means the company is enjoying a robust increase in sales.

6. **Four of the slices will be Hot Industries.** Hot industries really outperform their peers. In 1999, it was DOT COMs that rocketed up a return of 80%. In 2004, it was commodities, like copper. In 2005, Las Vegas Sands and other casinos were doubling in value. In 2007, clean energy earned almost 60 cents on the dollar, almost twice the returns of oil and gas (the 2nd highest performing industry). What will be the hot industry of tomorrow? You can learn to identify hot industries by utilizing my Stock Report Cards™ and Four Questions for Picking Winning Companies™ (from *You Vs. Wall Street*). You can also read my ezine to stay up to date. I

feature a Company of the Month each month and a Company of the Year annually. My 2012 Company of the Year, Jiayuan, posted 40% gains in under 60 days. My 2009 Company of the Year, U.S. Gold, posted up to 19 times gains!

7. **Underweight companies that were founded before 1980.** These tend to have significantly more pension and health care debt and obligations than newer companies, which provide 401Ks that employees manage themselves. The employers that are having trouble funding their pension plans (like auto manufacturers and airlines) are taking on a lot of debt to try and compete... Many have had to restructure, using the bankruptcy courts. Stocks are wiped out 100% during bankruptcy in 99.9% of all cases. If you want to do the research on how much a company owes in debt, pensions and other post-employment benefits (OPEBs), learn how to use the SEC Edgar database, where the full earnings reports are filed.

8. **What's safe?** If you are interested in bonds for the "safe" portion of your nest egg, you have to do extensive research first. Credit risk is driving the bond market. When a legacy company gives you a good interest rate, it is because they have a lot of debt, and there is greater risk than you might realize. Assume that

the higher the interest rate (and the higher the dividend), the higher the risk. Interest rates, from the central bank policy, should remain low until 2015, however, since credit risk is determining interest rates, don't think that your bonds and bond funds are fine. In general, the only bonds you want to keep are low-risk, short-term and low-debt – and those are probably not giving you enough return to make them attractive. However, the most important consideration for the "safe" side of your nest egg is that your money is not at risk of capital loss. If you need to educate yourself on bond basics, a good place to start is on the FINRA.org website. They have an excellent and extensive amount of information on Smart Bond Investing. If you have a lot of money on your "safe" side, and don't know what to do with it, read the Hard Assets, Real Estate and What's Safe? sections of this book for ideas.

9. **Rebalance at least once a year.** This is one of the most important aspects of the pie chart! It's simple, but critically important. Every year, print out the pie chart of what you actually own. Then draw a pie chart of how things should be allocated. Put a percent equal to your age safe. Overweight safe as needed and then slice the "at-risk" portion of the pie into ten funds, six by size and style and four *new* hot industries. (Real estate was

all the rage in 2005. Today, it's in the toilet. This year, if you turn on the television, you can't miss a gold advertisement, however, over the last 30 years, gold barely kept up with inflation, at 4.64% annualized gains.) When you compare what you have with what you should have, it is easy to see where you need to capture gains (i.e. sell), fill in the gaps (i.e. buy) and consider a new strategy altogether (certainly in the money you have "safe" and perhaps some of the "hot" industries).

10. **Don't include individual companies as part of your nest egg,** until you are as good at stock picking as Warren Buffett and Peter Lynch. Your nest egg is supposed to be money while you sleep, i.e. low risk and low maintenance. Individual companies require a lot of research before you buy, and frequent babysitting as to when is the right time to sell. If you are interested in investing in individual companies, then make sure you know how to pick a great company, determine the best buy in point, and take your profits early and often. Use the fun or educational money from your budget to purchase individual companies – not your nest egg. Reading *You Vs. Wall Street* will help tremendously with all of this, particularly the chapters on "Hitching Your Wagon to a Star" (which outlines my Four

Questions for Picking a Winner™), "Stock Report Cards™", the "3-Ingredient Recipe for Cooking up Profits™" and "Wall Street Secrets," which outlines buy low/sell high strategies.

Bottom Line

During these troubled economic times, of high debt, slow GDP growth and high unemployment, the most important thing for most people is overweighting safe and learning how to get safe now that bonds should come with a warning label (according to Warren Buffett). That is why I issued a new pie chart, overweighting 20% safe and offering new guidelines on what is safe, on October 1, 2012. (Within 45 days of that Get Safe warning, the Dow Jones Industrial Average dropped almost 1000 points.) That is also why we spend all of Day Three of my Investor Edu Retreat focused on safe, good yielding **hard** assets. **Hard assets will perform better than paper assets in the years to come.**

Take-Away Suggestions

1. Know what you own and how indebted that company or industry is as a whole. Underweight exposure to legacy companies that were founded more than thirty

years ago. Add in hot industries to increase performance.

2. Always keep a percentage equal to your age safe, and diversify the remaining money in your retirement account across ten funds that consider size, style, what is hot and underweight the bailouts and companies that are heavily in debt.

3. Rebalance at least once a year to capture your gains, make sure that you still have enough safe and update your hot industries. Re-evaluate your funds, in addition to reallocating your money.

Chapter 12: New Chips are Safer than Blue Chips

NASDAQ Continues to Beat the Dow.

By the end of 2012, the Dow was back to pre-recession levels, hitting a four-year high of 13,596 on Thursday, Sept. 20, 2012. Meanwhile, NASDAQ was on a rocket ship to the moon, more than doubling off of its March 2009 low. Since that time, NASDAQ has been hotter than gold, too.

Gold, NASDAQ & Dow Jones Industrial Average Performance

March 1, 2009 through December 14, 2012

Source: Money.MSN.com. Used with permission from Microsoft.

What does this mean to you?

1. **The Dow is Back, but not your Dough.**
2. **You're Still Vulnerable.**
3. **Don't Confuse a Bull Market With Wisdom**
4. **Now is the Time to Take Profits, Rebalance and Get Safe.**
5. **Now is the Time to Get Educated.**
6. **New Chips are Better Than Blue Chips.**

And here is additional information on each point.

1. **The Dow is Back, but not your Dough.** Losing half of your nest egg means it takes twice as long to get back to even. (Remember what I keep harping on: 10% return on $100,000 is $10,000, however 10% of $50,000 is only $5,000.) That means that in a volatile marketplace (what we have) during tough economic times (where we've been for the last decade), one of the most important things you must do is to keep enough money safe and to know what "safe" is, so you don't slide down too far. If you kept half safe before the Great Recession, your nest egg would be up by 50% (or more) since 2008 (by the end of 2012). If you didn't keep any money safe, then you were still underwater by 25%. Also, if you are relying on dividend-paying Blue Chips, your performance is much lower than that of the NASDAQ

New Chips, and your risk of principal loss could be greater than you know.

2. **You're Still Vulnerable.** If you lost too much in the Great Recession and didn't change anything, your nest egg is as vulnerable today as it was in 2008 (when I first warned to overweight your money safe). Why? We had even more debt in 2012 ($16 trillion) than the previous year, when the markets dropped 16% on the credit downgrade of the U.S. These crises are easy to avoid with a solid game plan. I warned to overweight safe again on October 1, 2012, due to the Debt Ceiling crisis that was scheduled to ensue immediately after the Presidential Election. By November 15, 2012, only 45 days after that warning, the Dow had lost almost 1000 points. Those who had too much at risk are crawling back to even again. Clearly, keeping enough safe is one of the most important aspects of investing in today's debt world.

How much of your nest age should you keep safe? Depends upon your age. If you are over 50 and you lost more than 20% in the Great Recession, your money house needs a makeover. You have too much at risk, at a time when you cannot afford to lose half of your nest egg. Even 25-year-olds could have limited their losses to 20% and earned gains on the safe side of their portfolio during the Great Recession, using my nest egg strategies. Again, keeping at least a percentage equal to your age safe and knowing what is safe in a Debt World are both critically important – just as important as avoiding the real estate bust in 2005 and the Dot Com bust in 2000. This is different than "market timing," or listening to scare tactics and putting all of your dough into gold.

The key is wisdom, diversification, smart selection and annual rebalancing. Things do change – quite dramatically – year to year. (Remember when MySpace was the most popular social network and teens watched TV instead of Hulu?) However, a solid game plan scores in bull and bear markets and gives you heat in the hot industries, without being burned by going all in.

3. **Don't Confuse a Bull Market With Wisdom.** If you are excited about the news on Wall Street and the recovery (somewhat) of your nest egg, it's important to remember that we were in a bull market between 2009 and 2012, and *everyone's nest egg has recovered.* Does this mean that your financial partner, who encourages you to buy and hold and wait it out is right? Definitely not. Buy and hold hasn't worked for a decade and will not work going forward. The Dow Jones Industrial Average has spent most of the New Millennium underwater and the NASDAQ has never fully recovered from the Dot Com Recession.

NASDAQ & Dow Jones Industrial Average Performance
January 1, 2000 through December 12, 2012

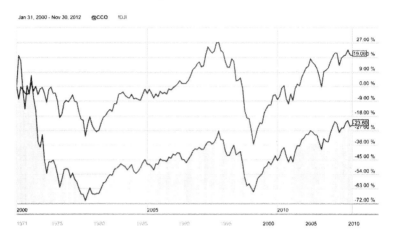

Source: Money.MSN.com. Used with permission from Microsoft.

Most money managers are either riding the waves of the market or performing worse than the indices. And if you have less than a million dollars, chances are that your financial partner has to service at least 500 other clients to make a living. You can do better with Modern Portfolio Theory, seasoned with a few of my tricks, and annual rebalancing – by far – than you will with buy and hold. If getting your financial advisor to implement your pie chart is a battle, then it's time to evaluate whether or not your CFP is a salesman. Read the chapter, "Brokers are Salesmen, Not Surgeons," in *You Vs. Wall Street* for tips on how to evaluate your financial partners, and the questions to ask to determine if they are really right for you. (They may have increased your net worth over the last three years merely because it was a bull market – not because their strategies were great.)

4. **October Has Become Harvest Season.** Another old school aphorism is "The Santa Rally." It used to be that 50% of the market gains were made in the last three months of the year – fueled by holiday spending. January was the top-performing month, so you could hang on to your gains for even more returns. The last decade has changed all of that.

Monthly Returns of the S&P500 (annualized % 1992 Through 2011

Month	20 years	10 years	5 years
January	0.0565	-1.63	-2.74
February	-0.62	-1.153	-2.13
March	1.14	0.82	**2.886**
April	**2.15**	**2.23**	**4.56**
May	0.7165	0.522	0.004
June	-0.57	-2.215	-3.56
July	0.13	-0.2712	**1.576**
August	-0.84	-0.11	-0.9274
September	-0.35	-0.8497	-0.076
October	1.953	1.366	-0.606
November	1.4435	0.801	-1.48
December	1.472	1.236	1.79

Source: Standard and Poor's data, Natalie Pace data crunch © 2012

As you can see, January and February have become two of the most dangerous months. December has remained strong, but is preceded by two months that can wipe out the December gains. In fact, the Spring Rally (March and April) has become far more reliable than the Santa Rally.

What turned the Santa Rally into Harvest Season? Debt... And taxes...

The Dow began its dismal 7,617 point drop – from 14,164 on October 6, 2007 to 6547 on March 9, 2009 – in October of 2007, when a spate of mortgage banks went belly-up. The U.S. credit was downgraded by Standard and Poor's in August of 2011, and investors didn't paint a smile back on until the end of November. The "Bush era" tax cuts are set to expire at the end of each year, creating additional uncertainty for investors this year, just like it did last year.

When I issued my Get Safe Now warning on October 1, 2012, I rightly warned that before the election, you'd hear a lot of rhetoric about jobs, unemployment, GDP growth and the stock market – mostly bad news and who is going to fix it faster. Investors would also be encouraged about modest job gains and GDP growth, however the going would be stop and go. Right after the election, the U.S. was set to hit the Debt Ceiling again. This was a big deal. If both parties didn't come together and fix the economic mess the U.S. was muddling through – with a plan for increased revenue *and* reduced government spending over the next decade – then the U.S. could be facing another debt downgrade from Moody's and Fitch, who still have the U.S. ranked at AAA. If the Debt Ceiling wasn't lifted, America wouldn't pay any bills.

Last year, partisan bickering in Congress meant that our representatives failed to meet the requirements to keep the Standard and Poor's AAA rating. They missed the mark by over $2 trillion. They knew what they needed to do and they missed the mark by half. The markets fell 16%. Can you afford to risk your future on partisan Congressional bickering?

5. **Now is the Time to Get Educated.** In our parent's generation, people worked at the same job their entire life and then retired with a good pension. Today, the average job will be eight years and employees have to manage their own self-directed 401ks. In other words, if you don't know what a healthy, balanced budget and nest egg look like, then you will suffer from poor fiscal health – and a very troubled, high-stress, worrisome life. If you do know and incorporate the Thrive Budget and my easy-as-a-pie chart nest egg strategy, you'll rest easy and enjoy great fiscal fitness, even with the rollercoaster economy of today.

Don't fear. You will not need to get a Ph.D. in economics, and you don't need to watch the financial news networks 24/7. You really only need to learn the ABCs of Money that you should have received in high school. Reading this book is an excellent start.

6. **New Chips are Better Than Blue Chips.** There is a fundamental reason why NASDAQ almost doubled the Dow between 2009 and 2012. Newer companies have a significant advantage in that they don't have to carry pensions and other post-employment benefits, like the legacy blue chips do. Many New Chips have no debt and a war chest of cash to boot. Learning how to avoid the Bailouts and add in the hottest companies and industries are key to performance in today's marketplace.

Here are more reasons why low debt equities, what I call New Chips, are safer than the legacy Blue Chips.

6 Reasons Silicon Valley is in a New Gold Rush.

1. **Colossal Debt versus Cash Rich.**
2. **Losing money vs. healthy profit margins and impressive sales growth.**
3. **Pension & OPEBs vs. 401ks.**
4. **Credit Risk vs. Cash Cows.**
5. **Stockton vs. Silicon Valley.**
6. **Dividends: The Higher the Yield, the Higher the Risk.**

And here's the 24-karat analysis.

1.   Colossal Debt versus Cash Rich.

One of the first things you'll notice if you do a New Chip versus Blue Chip Stock Report Card is that the New Chips have almost no debt, while most of the Blue Chips owe more money than the value of their company. JP Morgan Chase, American Express and General Electric all owe more than three times the value of their companies (as of November 2012). Meanwhile, Apple has zero debt with $117 billion in cash. Microsoft's cash on hand is $63 billion and Google has $44.6 billion, with very low debt levels (as of June 30, 2012, according to their respective earnings reports).

2.   Slim margins vs. healthy profits and impressive sales growth.

Many of the legacy Blue Chips have net profit margins below 10%, while the New Chips (established new, mega companies) boast margins that are double that or more. Apple and Google also had *sales growth* of 23% and 35% in 2012, making these colossally large companies growth stocks. By comparison, GE, Verizon and American Express all had tepid sales growth of less than 5%. JP Morgan had an earnings meltdown in the 2nd quarter of 2012, with sales off by 17%. Bank of America looked good on a year over year basis only because the 2nd quarter of 2011 was a complete disaster.

3. Pension & OPEBs vs. 401ks.

Many legacy Blue Chips began business a century ago, in a world where employees worked all of their lives and were then offered defined benefit plans in retirement. Today, the average life span of a job is eight years and everyone is in charge of managing their own 401k. A dramatic increase in life expectancy and the escalating costs of providing health care to retirees, who are living decades on their pensions, have crippled America's most enduring brands (legacy corporations) and municipalities. When corporations were making a promise to provide pensions and health care in retirement, the life span for a largely male workforce was near the age of retirement, meaning most people were passing away within a year, or before, of retiring, not expecting two decades of golden, labor-free years. The airline and auto industries have both used debt restructuring (bankruptcies) to get their debt and other post employment benefit obligations under control. (GM owed over $100 billion when it declared bankruptcy; Ford still owed that much in late 2012.) Other companies and municipalities (and even nations) are carrying unsustainable debt as they work toward a new system of having employees manage their own retirement plans. Nobody has figured out the best way to manage and pay for the $2.5 trillion spent on health care in the U.S. each year, although reducing our 34%

obesity rate would go a long way to mitigating the problem (source: CDC).

You might read this and feel sorry, or even angry, that the promises made to our grandparents will not be paid back in full. This is one of the core issues we must work through, *as a society and as a nation*, to solve our "debt problem." Individuals who are empowered and financially literate can do a much better job, going forward, of managing their own future. Legacy corporations clearly failed this mandate, although, in fairness, it's not entirely their fault. Living longer is a good thing, as long as you're not footing the bill.

4. Credit Risk vs. Cash Cows.

Six pre-recession Dow Jones Industrial Average component companies were bailed out, namely General Motors, AIG, Citigroup, Bank of America, American Express and JP Morgan Chase, representing 20% of the 30-company index. There are still three bailouts listed on the Dow Jones Industrial Average index (10%). Excessive debt, overleveraging, risky investments, pensions, Other Post Employment Benefits (like health care) and the inability to pay their bondholders on time were the core problems of the bailouts and bankruptcies of the past decade. Large Silicon Valley companies steered clear of the financial meltdown mess, as a general rule. They were busy making great products, instead of inventing new debt instruments to sale to unsuspecting buyers.

Even with the bailouts and the bankruptcy restructurings, debt is still a concern in the Blue Chips, but not in the New Chips. Most investors are not aware of the magnitude of the costs that legacy companies are spending on debt and retirees, many times borrowing from Peter to pay off Paul. Certainly few Washington Mutual bondholders, Lehman Bros. preferred stock holders, General Motors' stock and bondholders were fully aware of the risk associated with their investments. The question is, "Are you aware of the risk associated with your legacy Blue Chips today?"

5. Stockton vs. Silicon Valley.

Stockton, the city, declared bankruptcy on June 28, 2012. What happened? The city's booming real estate market went bust when speculators, who had been buying and flipping houses as fast as they could for a quick buck, realized the party was over and fled town. Silicon Valley, home to Stanford University, has incubated some of the world's most beloved companies and products – from the iPhone to Google to Intel and beyond. One area creates real value and products used around the world daily, while the other city was built on a get-rich-quick scheme. Knowing the difference is as easy as knowing what you use in your daily life.

That's not the complete story, however. There are a lot of old school company products that we use daily – from AT&T's networks to Home Depot's solar panels. That is why it is also important to complete the Stock Report Card™, to determine whether or not legacy costs are stifling growth, innovation and investment in the company you are invested in. GM was the leading auto manufacturer in the world in 2004. However when the American appetite turned to fuel-efficient cars, Toyota took the lead. With the legacy obligations and excessive debt, GM was unable to recreate and retool in time to compete. A large part of that was due to Toyota's vision. However, having the capital (human and financial) to retool factories was just as important. Instead of leading innovation and fuel efficiency in 2004, GM was embroiled in labor negotiations with its unions and debt negotiations with its bondholders – and borrowing money to meet payroll and other expenses while they tried to avoid bankruptcy and restructuring.

6. Dividends: The Higher the Yield, the Higher the Risk.

Over the last three years, the bulls have led the stock market, and dividend-paying stocks have rewarded investors. An important market aphorism is that one should never confuse a bull market with wisdom. When the markets go up, even troubled companies that are struggling with debt or to compete in a high-octane product environment can enjoy gains. Take a closer look at the debt and dividends of many Dow component companies and you will notice a very troubling correlation: the companies with the most debt are also the ones with the highest dividends. That means that investors should not have a false sense of complacency simply because their portfolios have done well in the last three years. If your nest egg lost more than 20% in 2008-2009, and you have not made any adjustments, you are just as vulnerable today as you were then – even more so if your dividend darlings are also debt-laden.

Bottom Line

New Chips are safer than Blue Chips. They are also earning two times the gains.

Take-Away Suggestions

1. If you lost money in the Great Recession, and you haven't made any changes, you could be even more vulnerable now than you were then. Getting safe means underweighting companies with too much debt – even if you love the dividends.

2. Companies founded before 1980 typically have more debt and other post employment benefit obligations than companies founded after 1980. This can be a

helpful guide, but if you want to know for sure, do a Stock Report Card™.

3. Large cap companies like Apple and Google have low debt, tens of billion in cash, double-digit sales growth and healthy profit margins. They are also very popular, so be sure that you are purchasing them at a good price. With the Wall Street rollercoaster, that is possible. Apple was down 25% off of its 52-week high on November 15, 2012, and if the market correction continued, it could go even lower. (My book *You Vs. Wall Street* offers tools and information on how to buy low and sell high.)

Chapter 13: Silicon Valley Spinster IPOs

5 Reasons It Was a Bad Idea to Buy Facebook, Zynga and Groupon at the IPO.

As I outlined in the previous chapter, newer companies have a significant advantage over legacy companies. Not only are their products (likely) more cutting edge and in demand. They don't have to deal with the legacy overhang, and associated debt. That doesn't mean, however, that every new company is a great investment – even if it is very popular with consumers. In fact, in 2011 and 2012, my biggest "hits" were warnings not to buy into the IPO fever of some very, very popular tech companies.

The problem with Facebook, Zynga & Groupon? These were Silicon Valley Spinster IPOs designed to marry off cash negative companies to unsuspecting investors, so that insiders could profit. (Groupon is a Chicago company.) These three companies still showed red flags for discerning investors in late 2012, which is why I plan to continue reporting so religiously on them in my ezine. These three companies have a lot of things going for them, including popularity with consumers;

however, they also have a lot of challenges they must overcome to operate profitably in the years to come.

Check out the Five Reasons it was risky to buy Facebook, Zynga and Groupon at the IPO below.

Five Ways to Spot a Great IPO vs. a Spinster IPO

	Qualities of Great Companies Going Public	Qualities of Spinster IPOs
1.	Outstanding Sales Growth	Inconsistent and/or Weak Sales Growth
2.	Impressive Profit Margins	Cash Negative and/or anemic profitability
3.	Diversified Revenue Stream	Struggling to figure out their profit plan
4.	Experienced Executive Team	Founder/CEO/chairman, green or with history of failures.
5.	Easy to Read Earnings Reports	Fuzzy Math Earnings Reports

When the Next Blue Chip Goes Public

Before I outline all of the concerns I have with Facebook, Zynga and Groupon, I want to give you an example of a great company going public.

At the time of its IPO, Google hit home runs in all of the assets you want to see in the next Blue Chip. It was the hottest water cooler conversation. Everyone wanted a piece of Google, and Google was making it possible for regular folks to do just that (at a time when it would have been far easier to do the typical road show for rich, experienced investors only). That was the first sign that the founders really had the investor's interest at heart. (If you want to travel back to 2004 to learn more about Google: The People's IPO, go to the archives of my ezines at NataliePace.com and click on volume 1, issue 48.)

Outstanding Sales Growth

In May of 2004, when Google filed its S-1 with the Securities and Exchange Commission, the company was doubling sales. It had gone from $500 million in sales in 2002 to $962 million in 2003. All indications were that this trend would continue, and it did. By August of 2005, Google's sales were $4.5 billion. Within four years, by October 2009, sales had exploded to $22.3 billion. In 2012, Google's sales were on track to hit $50 billion.

Impressive Profit Margins

Google was profitable, with 10% margins at the IPO. Over the next few years, the margins grew as high as 33% and then settled back in for a very respectable 22%.

Diversified Revenue Stream

Many analysts simply got this one wrong. They assumed that most of Google's sales were advertising, which was true, but that didn't make Google at the mercy of Madison Avenue. Why? Google was adopting the Yellow Pages market *and* Madison Avenue; the company was getting paid by Main Street *and* Wall Street. Mom and Pop Shop ads continued to fuel Google during the Great Recession, while other companies that were overly reliant on corporate marketing and advertising revenue (like the Las Vegas convention market) went belly up. Analysts also underestimated the mass migration from print to video advertising, which Google monetized through YouTube. Google launched Droid in 2010 and then acquired Motorola Mobility in 2011, even further diversifying its revenue stream into the smart phone market – another rapidly growing industry.

Experienced Executive Team

The product (initially just search) was developed by Google founders, Sergey Brin and Larry Page. However, the monetization vision was clearly conjured up by Dr. Eric Schmidt. Dr. Schmidt, a Silicon Valley veteran who had previously been chairman and CEO of Novell and CTO of Sun Microsystems, joined Google in 2001 as CEO and chairman. He came into a great startup with huge potential and transformed it into the worldwide global leader in search, smart phone and other technologies, with extraordinary sales growth and profitability. After a decade, Schmidt gave the CEO reins back to Larry Page, but he remains the executive chairman of Google.

Easy to Read Earnings Reports

Google emulated a lot of the best of Warren Buffett. They wanted to encourage long-term ownership of the shares, and discourage traders, so they vowed not to split the stock (which is why the share price is so high). Just like Berkshire Hathaway's earnings reports (before the Great Recession), Google's earning reports are designed to be simple to read and understand.

By contrast, most of the Class of 2011-2012 Internet IPOs was seriously deficient in those 5 key areas, with the exception of one.

Facebook

Facebook's sales growth in the second quarter of 2012 was 32% higher than the previous year, however, over the past six years, Facebook had only managed to get its revenue to a projected $4.33 billion. By comparison, over that same period, Google grew its sales from $5 billion to *$43.2* billion. Why? Zuckerberg was more interested in product than profits. He made this very clear in his letter to shareholders from the

Facebook S-1 filing, writing, "These days I think more and more people want to use services from companies that believe in something beyond simply maximizing profits. Simply put: we don't build services to make money; we make money to build better services." (Funny how Zuckerberg was the first to cash in a billion, however, during the first week of the Facebook listing on NASDAQ.)

Facebook reported a net loss of $157 million for the 2nd quarter of 2012. One of the biggest challenges facing Facebook is how to get paid for their service on mobile. Quite simply: there are no ads on mobile yet. Google innovated online advertising, away from the dreaded popup ad to the ingenious search and click ad, precisely because this was a priority. However, if Z's eye is not on profitability and he hasn't hired a Dr. Schmidt to get that ball rolling, who on the team is going to monetize the mobile market?

In his third quarter earnings call, Zuckerberg vowed that his team was now focused on monetizing mobile. So maybe there is hope going forward. Meanwhile, however, Google leads mobile ad innovation, as they did search ads in 2000. Google mobile revenue has more than tripled in just one year, going from $2.5 billion in 2011 to over $8 billion in 2012.

Even though Mark Zuckerberg has no experience managing a publicly traded company, he has almost complete control. Zuckerberg is the chairman and CEO, and he owns so much of Facebook that he "will be able to effectively control all matters submitted to [Facebook] stockholders for a vote, as well as the overall management and direction of [the] company," according to the amended S-1 filing of April 23, 2012. Sergey Brin and Larry Page may not have agreed with everything that Dr. Eric Schmidt initiated, but they were smart enough to put him in the driver's seat. It was a win-win-win for Google insiders, investors and web browsers alike.

So why did Facebook go public, if Zuckerberg doesn't really want anyone messing with his company? Because he was facing serious problems with his team if he didn't. Zuckerberg explains this clearly, writing, "We're going public for our employees and our investors. We made a commitment to them when we gave them equity that we'd work hard to make it worth a lot and make it liquid, and this IPO is fulfilling our commitment."

Zuckerberg neglected to mention that he'd be the first in line, even if it sent the Facebook share price into a tailspin. Almost $3.5 billion was cashed in by insiders in the first weeks of the IPO, sparking an implosion of the Facebook market value from $96.3 billion to $41.03 billion. Incidentally, insider selling continued at epic proportions in late 2012, even though the share price is worth less than half of its first days of trading. Board director Peter Thiel, a savvy Silicon Valley venture capitalist and the former CEO of PayPal, cashed in $401 million on August 17, 2012. He's sold over 85% of his shares, for almost a billion in profit.

Groupon

Groupon's CEO Andrew Mason is another founder/CEO, whose experience prior to Groupon was as a software developer with a degree in music. The team around Mason is impressive – with alumni from Google, eBay, Amazon and more. However, not one person on the executive team has been at Groupon longer than two years – mostly because the prior team (with a similar pedigree) jumped ship before the IPO (a big red flag!). (Go to my original article on Groupon, at NataliePace.com, volume 8, issue 12, for details.)

As of 2012, Groupon was still a cash-negative, revolving door, one-trick pony company, with stiff competition, including Google. Sales growth was flat on the year. For the record, Groupon did eke out a small profit in the 2nd quarter of 2012; however, the third quarter was back to cash negative.

Groupon's tricky way of accounting for "revenue" has been widely denounced, but if you missed the articles and are just checking out the earnings reports, it would be easy to be out of the loop on the double-speak and fine print. Groupon's "direct revenue" is less than 10% of the revenues they report (which are "third party"). If investors really knew that Groupon had zero direct revenue in 2011 (and only $84.6 million in the first half of 2012), far beneath the "reported" revenue of $1.6 billion in 2011, would Wall Street still have valued Groupon at $20 billion? It's easy to see why Groupon (as of the end of 2012) has not proven to be worth anything close to $20 billion – the high market valuation set in the first few days of trading on NASDAQ. By November of 2012, Wall Street valued Groupon at one-tenth of its early trading value, at under $2 billion.

If you were reading the fine print of the S-1 filing, you would have seen that this was also an IPO launched for insiders to get liquid, at your expense. Just a few months before the IPO, almost a billion in fresh capital was brought in, which was largely used to cash out old investors (to the tune of $809.8 million). Chairman Eric P. Lefkofsky cashed in $386 million of his Groupon stock at that time – just in time to be named to the annual *Forbes* Billionaire List. Groupon was criticized for this, as it would be in public investors' best interest if that capital was used to expand business and increase sales and profitability, not line the insiders' pockets with gold.

Zynga

Zynga is another company that has lost most of its market value after its IPO. At its zenith, Zynga was worth $12.5 billion.

By November 16, 2012, the company's value had slid to $1.72 billion.

One of the biggest concerns that investors have is that it is costing Zynga over half a billion a year to give away games for free. One of my biggest concerns for this company, in addition to the cash bleed, was the track record and poor staff polling of Zynga's chairman and CEO, Marc Pincus, both of which were highlighted in my Zynga IPO article in January 2012 (NataliePace.com, volume 9, issue 1). At the time of the IPO, Pincus scored one of the worst rankings of any CEO in Silicon Valley, with a measly 47% approval rating on GlassDoor, a popular Silicon Valley website, where employees can rank their companies and employers anonymously. Since then, the rating has improved to 64%, however, COO John Shappert left Zynga in October 2012 as did the general managers of MafiaWars, Cityville and Studio and the vice president of the mobile unit. The company advised the Securities and Exchange Commission of the departure of COO John Shappert, but did not release the information to the media or the general public. I received no response to my inquiry asking for confirmation or denial of the departures of the four key executives. Was that because there isn't someone answering the phone in the media department either? Or is it just an attempt to keep the news from the general public? Either are red flags...

Pincus' prior endeavor, Tribe, struggled to compete with Facebook and MySpace. After years of obscurity and near bankruptcy, Tribe was sold to Cisco for an undisclosed sum.

Sure, it's no small feat to hit $1.3 billion in sales – even if you're giving away games for free, to one of the largest online populations in the world (on Facebook), and burning through over half a billion dollars to get there. With a chunk of his leadership team gone and those remaining cashing in their options as fast as they can – even at fire sale prices – Pincus has his work cut out for him not to burn through his remaining cash in the next two years. Online gaming is a competitive, fickle space. Remember when everyone was in a poker room, instead of out on the farm?

Palo Alto Networks

Palo Alto Networks was one of the recent Silicon Valley IPOs of that period to show qualities of a great company going public. Revenue growth was outstanding. 2012 revenue was double that of 2011. Profit margins are going to be healthy, once the company gets out of R&D mode. The executive team, particularly the CEO, is highly qualified. And the communication to investors is clear and easy to understand. The only reason this company was not featured on my Hot List in 2012 was that its shares are trading at their all-time high.

Popular Does Not Mean Profitable

The simple truth is that when companies have been attracting top-tier talent with massive stock options and burning through hundreds of millions in venture capital for more than three years, they have very few options to keep operating. If they don't turn paper equity into real money, they'll lose their team, and if they don't come up with a better profitability plan, they'll have no dough on hand to meet payroll.

Bottom Line

If a company is cash negative and has burned through hundreds of millions (or more) in investment capital, but is very popular with the masses, as Facebook, Groupon and Zynga were before their IPOs, one of the easiest ways to continue operating and secure the capital to do so is to satisfy the liquidity demands of the insiders with an IPO. You, the public investor, might get stuck with stock worth a fraction of its IPO valuation, but the company buys a few more years to figure everything out. I'm not sure that the insiders are laughing all the way to the bank. The feeling is probably more of a "Whew." But they are at the bank. With your dough.

Take-Away Suggestions

1. Read *You Vs. Wall Street*, particularly the chapters on the 3-Ingredient Recipe for Cooking Up Profits™, Stock Report Card™ and Hitch Your Wagon to a Star, to learn how to identify great IPOs from spinster IPOs.

2. Popular does not mean profitable! You can't just buy stock in the companies and products you love. If you're not willing to do the research, then don't own the stock.

3. The track record of the CEO can be very informative with regard to a new company going public. (Established companies just don't have inexperienced founder/CEOs running the show. Larry Page was mentored for a decade under Dr. Eric Schmidt before he was given the reins at Google.)

Part 5: What's Safe?

Chapter 14: Bond Defaults in a Debt World.

The Federal Open Market Committee "currently anticipates" (not promises, anticipates) rock bottom interest rates through mid-2015. That calmed bond investors, in my view a little too much, particularly with respect to the safe side of their nest egg. If you look closely at the pie charts from the Stocks section of *The ABCs of Money*, you'll see that I've listed bonds, bond funds, treasury bills and bailed out blue chips as vulnerable, and consider hard assets, cash positive, income producing income property (apartment buildings or shopping malls), Australian bonds and consumer staples businesses (think Chipotle's, dry cleaners, car washes, etc.) to be safer.

Why do I list bonds and bond funds (and Treasury bills) as vulnerable, when the Federal Reserve Board has made such a promise? Because the biggest concern in the bond market today is not interest rate risk. Credit risk – not FOMC policy – is determining the yield of bonds in today's market. Also, in the coming years, hard assets will perform much better than all paper assets.

As we've seen in the credit crises of European Union countries like Portugal, Ireland, Italy, Greece and Spain (PIIGS), the Central Bank's idea of interest rates is one thing and the market's idea is quite another. Marginal lending rates of the European Central Bank are rock bottom, just like the U.S. Meanwhile 10-year Greek bonds would have had to pay interest rates above 20% to attract any investors before the bailouts.

So, even though treasury yields in the United States actually declined in the wake of the Standard and Poor's credit downgrade of August 5, 2011, it is important to understand that as credit concerns rise, interest rates rise, too. The U.S. looks a lot better, by comparison, than PIIGS. We are still the largest economy in the world, with an enviable piece of land, friendly neighbors, an educated population, great universities and we are one of the world's leaders in inventing the products of tomorrow. Our unemployment is much lower than Greece and Spain. The assets of the U.S. are not going to go away quickly, however, our $16 trillion dollar debt will scare off investors, if we don't fix that. Meanwhile, some U.S. corporations and municipalities are already feeling the squeeze by bond investors.

Our bonds and interest rates are being kept artificially low by policy manipulation. We are buying our own debt – borrowing from ourselves. That money is coming from funds that will need to be paid back, including trusts of Social Security, Unemployment, Disability, Federal Employees, Hospital Insurance and more.

Because credit risk is the primary concern, the economic recovery and GDP growth of the U.S. lies largely in the hands of politicians, who, so far, have failed quite miserably at the task of reducing the U.S. debt and balancing the budget. In August of 2011, Congressional leaders missed the mark of $4 trillion in budget savings over a ten-year period – which was needed to avoid the Standard and Poor's credit downgrade – by almost half. Federal of Reserve Chairman Ben Bernanke warned of the high stakes of taking on too much debt in his speech on August 26, 2011 at Jackson Hole, Wyoming, saying, "Without significant policy changes, the finances of the federal government will inevitably spiral out of control, risking severe economic and financial damage." Bernanke further outlined what is needed to promote long-term growth, saying, "To allow the economy to grow at its full potential, policymakers must work to promote macroeconomic and financial stability; adopt effective tax, trade, and regulatory policies; foster the development of a skilled workforce; encourage productive investment, both private and public; and provide appropriate support for research and development and for the adoption of new technologies." Bernanke also warned that "The increasing fiscal burden that will be associated with the aging of the population and the ongoing rise in the costs of health care make prompt and decisive action in this area all the more critical."

So, what happens when politicians fail to do their job, and kick the can of reform and budget savings (which includes spending cuts, entitlement reform and revenue) down the road? Fortunately or unfortunately, we have many recent examples that should warn us of the perils of procrastination.

PIIGS: European Countries in Credit Crisis

Portugal, Ireland, Italy, Greece and Spain have all made headlines over the past few years for having high debt in relation to their GDP. These countries have had difficulty raising money to pay their bills, and thus had to raise interest rates to attract any bond buyers at all. Below I outline what happened to bond rates in two of those countries, as the crises escalated.

Spain

Spain's 10-year bond rate has risen 48% over the last three years, from 3.99% in 2009 to 5.87% in November of 2012. You might think that's still pretty low, until you consider that the price Spain has to pay just to borrow more money has almost doubled, which escalates the debt, which pushes the interest rates even higher.

Greece

10-year Greek bond yields were at 37% in March of 2012 – before the European Union bailouts – a price Greece was unable and unwilling to pay.

Just three years ago, in July of 2009, Greek 10-year notes offered 4.58% yield. Investors who purchased Greek bonds a few years ago got stuck with a very bad investment. As part of the Greek bailout package, a bond swap deal was struck that wiped out 70% of the value of existing bonds. The Greek bond crisis was at the heart of the MF Global bankruptcy.

U.S. Municipal Bonds

Certain segments of the U.S. population are experiencing the same kind of scenario. In Stockton, California, the city is trying to walk away from $124 million in debt from pension-obligation bonds it floated in 2007. According to a statement by Assured Guaranty, who stands to lose if the deal is approved, 83% of the principal of bondholders would disappear. (Imagine investing in a muni bond where 83 cents of every dollar you invested was never paid back!)

AIG was bailed out. Washington Mutual, Lehman Bros., Bear Stearns and Countrywide – all darlings of Wall Street before the real estate crash and the Great Recession – turned out to be horrible credit risks. General Motors and Chrysler bondholders had to go through bankruptcy, as have most investors of legacy airline bonds.

Clearly, even though we have rock bottom Fed rates, it is critically important to understand the credit risk of your bonds! They may not be as safe as you think.

Here are a few ways to do that:

1. Find out how much debt the municipality or corporation has. Is it AAA rated? Or is it deeply underwater? Check the SEC filings for the total debt, the financial websites for the debt to equity ratio and the ratings agencies for the credit rating. It's a great idea to do a

Stock Report Card™ and line up the competition as well. (Learn more about Stock Report Cards in my book *You Vs. Wall Street.*)

2. Cross reference the debt with the income. How much money is coming in to pay back the debt? Where is the money coming from? Is the source of the income reliable? Are the sales more or less this year from last year? Use the Four Questions from *You Vs. Wall Street* to help you in this analysis.

3. Cities like Stockton and Bakersfield were booming during the real estate run, and crashed when the boom came to a screeching halt. What is the underlying product or service of the municipality or corporation? Is it something people want and need, like Apple products or online travel sites? Or is it something that is falling out of favor, like an old school travel agency, or an oil well that has run dry?

Corporate Bonds

Doing that sober analysis will prevent you from falling into the mindset that your favorite company is just better than the others. Investors thought American Airlines was better off than all of the airlines that declared bankruptcy (virtually all of the "legacy" airlines). However, the truth wasn't that American Airlines was better or didn't have the same challenges. The company just able to hang on longer. American Airlines finally fell on Nov. 29, 2011 and was still struggling a year later to put a deal in place that would allow it to emerge from bankruptcy.

General Motors lost money for six years – totaling $88 billion – before filing for bankruptcy protection in 2009. Think Ford is in much better shape? Think again. Ford had over $100 billion of debt in 2012. That is a huge drag, particularly when the company had lower sales in 2012 than in 2011.

If you want to own any type of bond in today's Debt World, it is critically important that you evaluate the debt and credit risk. Remember one rule of thumb: the higher the interest, the higher the risk. If the interest rate is more than a few points above the marketplace (which is now at zero) and/or the debt of the issuer is a big concern, your bond is not *safe*. It is "at risk", and sometimes even "speculative".

So, what Happens When Interest Rates Rise?

Interest rates on bonds can rise due to credit risk (as we saw in Greece, Spain and other countries and municipalities) or interest rate risk (as will happen once the Federal Reserve Board increases interest rates).

1. The value of existing bonds goes down.

No one is going to want to buy your 4.58% Greek bond and have to hold it for eight years, when the current 10-year bonds are offering 14.6%. That is the primary reason that bondholders agreed to a swap that cost them so much money. Even with that kind of return, most people are avoiding this bond altogether, as you can see below.

2. Liquidity dries up

In 2009, Greek bonds were traded in high demand on the electronic secondary securities market (HDAT). Bond volume in July of 2009 was 18.19 billion euro, with 57.3% buyers and 42.7% sellers. Trading volume in July of 2011 for Greek government bonds had dried up to just 131 million euro, with 65% sellers and only 35% buyers. By November 2012, there were no buyers and bondholders were swapping out their current bonds for ones worth a lot less, as part of an emergency bailout deal.

3. Principal is at risk

In the event that a bondholder is forced to sell to pay other bills, then s/he will have to lower the price of the bond in order to attract buyers. In that scenario, the bondholder loses a substantial portion of the principal, in addition to the interest. In the case of bankruptcy, the bondholder will typically be offered some kind of deal for at least the principal of the bond, however, that deal might still be pennies on the dollar, as is the case in Stockton, California. It also might be stock, which can fluctuate dramatically in share price, as was the case at General Motors and Chrysler.

4. Hold to term is possible if there isn't a default.

It is possible to get your principal back if you hold your bond to term and the borrower doesn't default. There are a lot of ifs in that sentence. This is why you must evaluate the credit risk of all of your bonds.

5. Bond Funds

When interest rates rise the value of the bond fund will go down, too. So, bond funds are not safe in the Debt World either. In fact, because bond funds are traded on the stock market, the tide on bond funds can turn even more rapidly than the bond market.

Credit Risk is more important than Fed Policy

In a world where credit risk, not interest rate policy, is determining bond yields, income, debt, pensions, other financial obligations and husbandry determine the future. Countries and companies with high debt have to adopt a sound business plan to **increase revenue and economic growth while at the same time making dramatic cuts on spending,** in order to keep their credit scores high. (We discussed that this is the same plan you have to have in your own household, if your debt is too high.) Just as you want your company to be innovating and competing in a fast global economy, the nation must do so as well. When you are evaluating corporations, municipalities and countries, you should be examining both sides of that equation – revenue now and going forward and a sustainable spending plan that allows the company to compete, without breaking the bank.

Those countries that adopt "austerity" measures to cut spending and to reduce their debt to GDP ratios risk picketing, rioting and flash mobs, as we've seen in Europe. Those countries that don't make the necessary spending cuts and reform risk a financial meltdown, as we've seen in Greece (and the PIIGS nations). Nobody in trouble can afford to borrow money at 30% interest rates.

Protect Yourself Now

The next chapter provides even more guidelines on how to protect yourself and evaluate the fiscal health and debt load of any nation, municipality and/or corporation before you loan your money. Essentially, you want to determine the likelihood of getting your principal back in full, and having the interest payments made on time. As Roy Rogers once said, "I'm more concerned about the return *of* my money than the return *on* my money."

Bottom Line

We live in a Debt World that is full of credit risk. Staying ahead of the game is not as hard as you think. Most of the information and data that you need to determine how risky your bond holdings are can be obtained with a few clicks and a well-defined search, using the tools you'll find in my books.

Take-Away Suggestions

1. Bonds are not as safe as you think, particularly in today's Debt World. Defaults, swaps and bankruptcies are occurring and bondholders are losing money in those cases.

2. Use Stock Report Cards™ and the Four Questions for Picking a Winner™ to evaluate whether the bonds you have are worth the risk. These tools are found in my book, *You Vs. Wall Street*. The next chapter will also help you separate the bonds you want to keep from those that are more at risk.

3. Credit risk, not interest rate risk, is driving the bond market today.

Chapter 15: Separating the Brides From the Bailouts

Which of your holdings do you want to stay married to?

Are Bonds Safe?

The answer is yes and no. As I outlined in the previous chapter, if you purchase a bond, hold it for the duration of the term, receive an interest rate that pays you a nice income and the borrower doesn't default, then bonds are safe. However, there are a lot of ifs in that sentence. And those ifs can slide down a slippery slope into illiquidity, payment delays and/or default in times like we are seeing today.

There are two main risks in bonds, and both are present in today's bond market (even with the Federal Reserve Board's notice that interest rates will likely stay low until 2015).

1. **Credit Risk:**

In short, the higher the interest rate, the higher the risk that you are taking on. If most bonds are in the 2% range and you are offered an 8% rate, then you need to seriously examine the income, debt and outlook of the entity you are lending money to. As Ted Hampton, an analyst for Moody's Investor Service pointed out last year, "Unfunded pension liabilities have become more pronounced and unmanageable. In Illinois, they literally can't pay for them. They are issuing bonds two years in a row." In the previous chapter, we looked at Stockton, California, where the pension bonds are in default.

What happens in the worst-case scenario? Bankruptcy and/or default. You know about Chrysler, General Motors, Delta Airlines, U.S. Air and United Airlines, but did you know that cities and counties can declare bankruptcy, too? (States can't.) New York City restructured in 1975, Cleveland in 1978 and Orange County, California in 1994. Bondholders negotiate a settlement in bankruptcy court, but typically receive far less than they are owed, far later than they were promised. Stockton, California pension bond investors may really get screwed.

2. **Interest Rate Risk:**

When interest rates rise, the value of your bond goes down (and vice versa). Interest rates in the U.S. are at rock bottom, lower than inflation, which means that at some point, they will have to rise. In fact, Canada, China and the European Union did raise interest rates in 2011, over concerns of inflation. As we saw in the previous chapter, the riskiest bond issuers are forced to raise rates, due to the credit risk, to attract new borrowers, even if the central bank policy is rock bottom.

Keeping on the Safe Side of Bonds

Today, we have an environment where countries, municipalities and corporations are carrying very high debt, and many are operating at a budget deficit (borrowing to pay bills). Cities and counties are using bankruptcy to get bondholders to accept less than they were promised. Even though states can't declare bankruptcy, they can default on their bonds, so you can't have blind faith in your state-issued bonds either.

Below are six considerations to help you evaluate the fiscal health of your bond portfolio.

1. **Fiscal Health:** Look into the debt and revenue of the underlying country, corporation, municipality or revenue stream that is securing the bond. Don't simply rely on rating agencies (although that's a good start). Make your own assessment. Safe bonds have reasonable debt, solid revenue growth and are borrowing to create a better product or expand production. Risky bonds have massive debt and are borrowing more to pay bills.

2. **Bailouts vs. Brides**: Separate the bonds that are high yielding (above 5%) from the low-yield bonds. If you have a low-yield bond that passed the fiscal health exam (#1 above) that is maturing in 2-3 years, you can throw that into the bride pile. If you have a low-yield bond that is longer term and has serious fiscal issues, you may be looking at a future bailout and/or default. Remember: if you are going to take on a lot of risk, you want to be rewarded for it. Examine the debt, sales and income of your long-term and high yield bonds to determine if you wish to take on that level of risk. Exclude this bond from your "safe" money. If you're able to sell your risky bonds for a good price today, you may be glad that you got out early – even if it takes a year or two for you to know that you were right.

3. **Tax-free Muni's**: Do an extensive analysis of any Municipal Bonds you are holding, particularly of the debt. According to Dr. Marc Miles, a global strategist and the former senior economist of the Heritage Foundation, the problems in Greece, Ireland and Portugal are similar to the problems in California, Arizona, Illinois, Michigan, Kentucky, Louisiana, and New Jersey. Include union/pension funding/benefits and other post employment benefit obligations and debt in your evaluations.

4. **Separate the Googles from the GMs**: Evaluate your corporate bonds using the Stock Report Card and by asking the Four Questions. (These are both outlined in my book, *You Vs. Wall Street*.) With the high profile bankruptcies (Lehman Brothers, Blockbuster, airlines, automakers, Kodak, Hostess and more) and bailouts (all of the major U.S. banks + AIG and more), you should be on high alert that there are a number of legacy corporations that have a heavy load of debt, pension and Other Post Employment Benefit obligations. Quarterly earning reports include the pensions, debt and OPEBs at the end of the report *in the fine print*. You may have to go to the Edgar database of SEC.gov in order to ensure that you are completely aware of the load the company is carrying.

Companies that are heavily burdened with debt and obligations, almost to the point of bankruptcy, can still turn a profit for the quarter, so don't rely just on the headlines. Debt doesn't count against earnings until it's due, which is why a company like GM could report something positive about sales, instead of sending out a press release on its upcoming liquidity problems.

5. **Water Revenue versus Missing Revenue**: Evaluate the Revenue Bonds considering the source of the revenue.

Ask yourself, "Will this particular revenue stream be strong if we slide back into a recession?" In tough times, people prioritize their spending. The water bill may be a staple, while the nuclear power plant bond may be a bad bet, particularly given the Japanese nuclear disaster. According to PublicBonds.org, "The largest default in the history of the municipal bond market was the Washington Public Power Supply System's (WPPSS) default on $2.25 billion in bonds. WPPSS launched a risky program to build five nuclear power plants in the 1970s to supply electricity to the Pacific Northwest. Only one of the five planned nuclear plants was ever completed."

6. **Bond Funds.** Funds, in general, are a way to overcome risk by spreading your exposure across multiple municipalities and corporations. However, when an entire industry comes under attack, the fund will lose value. Real estate funds lost half (or more) of their value between 2007 and 2009. European bond funds have been one of the worst places to be over the last few years.

Bottom Line

In general, there are safer investments today than paper assets – like cash-positive hard assets. You need to be smart about the headwinds in the bond marketplace. If you do wish to hold bonds, keep the term short, the credit-worthiness high and scrutinize your holdings like a father evaluating the first date of his only daughter.

Take-Away Suggestions

1. Triple tax-free bonds are not attractive if you are at risk of losing principal.
2. Bonds, in general, are not "safe" when interest rates are rising – regardless of whether it is due to credit risk or interest rate risk. So find other ways of protecting the safe side of your nest egg.
3. Keep the terms of your bonds short and the credit worthiness high.

Chapter 16: Is the U.S. the Next Greece?

Discover some countries with low debt and good prospects.

When you consider that the U.S. has a $16 trillion debt, then you might be worried that the United States is headed down the path to Greece (in the words of Governor Mitt Romney, during his Presidential campaign). There is no doubt that better husbandry is in order for the U.S., just as it is in all of the developed world. If everyone were willing to cut back, then the impact on any one group becomes lower. As John Heywood writes, "Many hands make light work."

However, spending cuts are only half of the necessary strategy. Think of your own budget. Let's say that you are in the hole because you were out of work. Getting a job would go a long way to balancing the budget. Or, if you had your hours cut, then taking a part-time job might fix the hole as well. In the same way, the U.S. has to be concerned with income. Creating the products of tomorrow, which keep U.S. citizens gainfully employed, is a big piece of the fix. We'd be in real trouble if our primary exports were typewriters and landline telephones. So, if we know that gas prices are headed higher due to dramatically increased demand from China and India, then creating fuel-efficient cars is important. If we project that the Fukushima Daiichi nuclear disaster will curtail the public appetite for nuclear power, then having the U.S. lead in clean energy product innovation becomes very important, too.

Finally, just as we have to address the big spending in our own budget to balance it, we must fix the floods in the national budget. Over the past decade, our second largest trade deficit has been to OPEC. Oil imports are down to a 15-year low and oil production is up under President Obama. However, the U.S. still spent more than $421 billion on oil and petroleum imports in 2011. These are subtractions to our GDP growth in the same way that driving an expensive gas-guzzler can ruin your own budget.

I'll outline the debt of the U.S. and other countries below, with special emphasis on the safest countries in the world (lower debt). However, before I do, let's take a look at the income side. To our benefit, the U.S. exports technology products and services, food and beverages, consumer goods, capital goods and more. Wall Street is one of the world's financial centers. Silicon Valley is the world's leading technology innovator. We still have a strong auto manufacturing export business. We need to stay on top in these industries and anticipate the emerging markets of tomorrow (which will include clean energy) to compete in a global economy. I focus on this because income is where a lot of the PIIGS nations are missing the mark.

Income in PIIGS Nations

A few years ago, pigs were just farm animals. Today, PIIGS are European nations that no one wants to lend money to (namely Portugal, Ireland, Italy, Greece and Spain). Their debt has a stench, which keeps investors at bay, forcing these countries to borrow money at interest rates that only make the problem worse. Most of these countries have adopted "austerity" measures – high taxes – but many of them are still falling far too short on the income side – GDP growth. Spain and Greece have 25% unemployment – with almost half of young adults under 25 without a job. By comparison, U.S. unemployment was 7.9% in October 2012.

Greece's primary industry is tourism. Tourism is also a big industry in Spain. The problem is that tourism suffers severely in recessions, meaning these countries need a more diversified revenue stream. Meanwhile, the strongest economies in the eurozone are leaders of industry. Germany is known for engineering. Exports include machinery, vehicles, chemicals and household equipment.

So, when you think of how to diversify internationally, while also protecting your 401k, IRA, annuity and pension from the Eurozone crisis (really the developed world crisis), there remain two top considerations – debt and income. In my analysis below, I've lined up the countries with the lowest debt, and then included the freedom ranking (which assesses everything from property rights to corruption and beyond), Standard and Poor's foreign currency rating, GDP growth and unemployment. I've also thrown in the United States, Canada, select European countries, Singapore and Japan, for comparison purposes.

Debt & Freedom by Country

Country	Debt to GDP Ratio	Freedom Ranking	Foreign Currency Rating	Unemployment	GDP Growth
Estonia	5.80	16.	AA-	27.3%	7.6%
Kuwait	6.80	71.	AA	2.2%	8.2%
Qatar	**8.90**	**25.**	**AA**	**0.4%**	**14.1%**
Saudi Arabia	9.40	74.	AA-	10.9%	7.1%
Chile	**9.40**	**7.**	**A+**	**6.6%**	**5.9%**
Hong Kong	**10.10**	**1.**	**AAA**	**3.4%**	**5.0%**
Luxembourg*	20.40	13.	AAA	5.7%	1.6%
Australia	**30.30**	**3.**	**AAA**	**5.1%**	**2.1%**
New Zealand	33.70	4.	AA	6.5%	1.3%
Taiwan	**34.90**	**18.**	**AA-**	**4.0%**	**4.4%**
Sweden	**36.80**	**21.**	**AAA**	**7.5%**	**4.0%**
Czech Republic	40.70	30.	AA-	8.5%	1.7%
China	43.50	138.	AA-	6.5%	9.2%
Emirate of Abu Dhabi	43.90	35.	AA	2.4%	5.2%
Denmark	46.50	11.	AAA	6.1%	0.8%
Norway	48.40	40.	AAA	3.3%	1.5%
Finland*	49.00	17.	AAA	7.8%	2.7%
Switzerland	52.40	5.	AAA	2.8%	1.9%
The Netherlands*	64.40	15.	AAA	4.4%	1.1%
United States" (see note below)	69.40	10.	AA+	7.9%	1.8%
Austria	72.10	28.	AA+	4.2%	2.7%
United Kingdom	79.50	14.	AAA	8.1%	0.8%
Germany	81.50	26.	AAA	6%	3.1%
Canada	83.50	6.	AAA	7.5%	2.4%
France	85.50	67.	AA+	9.2%	1.7%
Singapore	118.20	2.	AAA	2.0%	4.9%
Japan	208.20	22.	AA-	4.6%	-0.8%

*on Negative Watch

Source: Foreign Currency Ratings provided by Standard and Poor's. Debt to GDP, Unemployment and GDP growth data from CIA.gov The World Factbook. Freedom Ranking from The 2012 Index of Economic Freedom, a publication of the Heritage Foundation, in partnership with The Wall Street Journal.

The U.S. debt to GDP numbers exclude debt issued by individual US states, as well as intra-governmental debt; intra-governmental debt consists of Treasury borrowings from surpluses in the trusts for Federal Social Security, Federal Employees, Hospital Insurance (Medicare and Medicaid), Disability and Unemployment, and several other smaller trusts; if data for intra-government debt were added, "Gross Debt" would increase by about one-third of GDP.

The 6 Mostly Free countries (based on *The Index of Economic Freedom*) that I've bold highlighted above, have less than 50% debt to GDP ratio, GDP growth above 2%, low unemployment and an A sovereign rating by Standard and Poor's (or above). These countries are namely Qatar, Chile, Hong Kong, Australia, Taiwan and Sweden. I did not highlight Abu Dhabi and Finland. While the United Arab Emirates has made progress toward freedom and free markets, the UAE still restricts foreign investment and the judicial system is subject to political influence, according to the editors of *The 2012 Index of Economic Freedom*. The UAE has been hit very, very hard by the real estate decline. And, the unemployment rate excludes the important fact that most women are still classified as "household workers." Finland was riding too high on unemployment and debt and too weak on GDP growth to include.

The main exports of the strongest countries are: oil (Qatar), copper and other commodities (Chile), trade and finance (Hong Kong), natural resources (Australia), electronics and machinery (Taiwan) and timber, iron ore and engineering (in Sweden). Qatar was the first Arab country to grant women the right to vote (in 1999), but it is surrounded by unrest in the Middle East and the Arab Spring and it is difficult to invest in Qatar without getting exposure to the more volatile nations as well. Which leaves Chile, Hong Kong, Australia, Taiwan and Sweden as the cream of the world.

According to the World Fact Book, Australia could return to budget surpluses as early as 2015. Australia was one of the first advanced economies to raise interest rates, with seven rate hikes between October 2009 and November 2010, offering the most attractive, low risk interest rates in the world. One of the easiest ways to invest in Australia is through a bond fund or by investing directly in a bank. Banks in Australia are offering the highest yields, at 6.70 for Westpac (symbol: WBK). Always consider price when investing in any individual stock or fund! The beauty about volatile markets is that patient buyers are usually afforded a good buy price.

Kuwait and Saudi Arabia have very low debt, but are not very business or investor friendly. World leaders, like the U.K., U.S., Germany and Canada, are free, stable economies with great credit ratings, but have debt to GDP ratios that are as high as Spain's. That doesn't mean you don't want to invest in these great, free countries, particularly in some of the solid companies that are located in them. I've already discussed the difference between New Chips and Blue Chips. But it does mean that sovereign bonds are more vulnerable, low yielding and at risk of becoming devalued, due to the high debt, slow GDP growth and the potential for inflation. (These facts continue to support my heavy emphasis on holding hard assets in the developed world.)

The risk in some of the "developing" world isn't that they *can't* pay you back, but that they won't. The funds might be seized by a megalomaniacal dictator, or the government might take over private companies "for the public good." The risk in the developed world is that they are promising to pay everybody back and some people, including pensioners, are already getting shortchanged. Stockton, California is but one example. Many workers have taken dramatic haircuts in their salary and benefits as a result of their company restructuring through Chapter 11. Too many promises of payment and too little money to go around are at the heart of the problems in all of the developed world.

Excessive Debt in PIIGS Nations

Country	Debt to GDP Ratio	Freedom Ranking	Foreign Currency Rating
Greece	165.40	119.	CCC
Iceland	130.10	27.	BBB-
Ireland	107.00	9.	BBB+
Italy	120.10	92.	BBB+
Portugal	103.30	68.	BB
Spain	68.20	36.	BBB+

Source: Foreign Currency Ratings provided by Standard and Poor's. Debt to GDP ratios from CIA.gov The World Factbook. Freedom Ranking from The Index of Economic Freedom.

So, how do you invest in safer securities from Chile, Hong Kong, Australia, and Sweden? It's easier than you might think, thanks to fund companies, like Pimco, iShares, Morgan Stanley and Wisdom Tree.

Pimco is one of the largest, most established investment management firms in the world, with over $1.77 trillion in assets under management. It has been in business for four decades. Pimco has a new Australia bond fund, as does Wisdom Tree.

Equity Opportunities in Low Debt Countries

It's important to understand that equity funds (stocks) should not be considered as part of your "safe" allocations because stock markets can be volatile, even when companies and countries are good investments, particularly today. So, if you think owning stock in these countries might add some heat to your returns, use them as one or more of your hot slices of your nest egg pie chart. Be sure to buy at a great price. Have a plan to capture your gains and re-evaluate whether they will remain *hot* next year.

Even though these countries look like the strongest in the world, don't go overboard with your investments. Don't throw all of your "safe" side into one bond fund. Remember to consider hard assets for your safe money, too. The markets are bought and sold by people and not everyone has the done the analysis I just did. If bonds and bond funds become vulnerable, there may be some "throwing out the baby with the bath water," i.e. getting rid of their solid bonds, too.

For ongoing updates, information and news, check out my ezine and Hot News on Cool Stocks Report at NataliePace.com. I do a market update twice a month and publish a monthly ezine there.

Bottom Line

There are low-debt countries with good export prospects that are providing great investment opportunities, even today. The key is to stay on top of the changing dynamics (rebalance your nest egg portfolio at least once a year), and to purchase any bond, fund or stock at a great price.

Take-Away Suggestions

1. The six most attractive countries in the world, with low debt, stable or strong GDP growth and a solid "freedom" ranking, are Qatar, Chile, Hong Kong, Australia, Taiwan and Sweden.

2. An easy way to have a good yield is to purchase stock in an Australian bank, where yields are still above 6%. Remember to purchase for a good price!

3. If you purchase a stock (equity) fund, consider it a "hot" slice of your nest egg pie chart. If you purchase a bond fund from a low debt, high-yielding country, it can be part of your safe allocation. Don't put all of your safe money there, however. Diversification remains very important, and hard assets should perform better than paper assets in the coming years.

Chapter 17: What's Safe?

10 Things to Know About Your Bank, Annuity and Brokerage.

We live in a post-bailout world, full of stress tests and fancy accounting. In short, the banks and a few insurance companies screwed up so much that if we had not bailed them out, we wouldn't have any. Despite that, however, many investors are seduced into buying "safe" bank and insurance products from the very companies that couldn't be trusted just a few short years ago. Sometimes the fine print of the products are so confusing that even the company salesmen get it wrong. On November 15, 2012, the SEC fined Massachusetts Mutual Life Insurance Company for failing to sufficiently disclose the potential negative impact of a "cap" it placed on a complex annuity product that investors were planning to use for retirement. The SEC iterates that MassMutual removed the "cap" in question before any investors were harmed. However, according to the SEC, when the cap was in place, "In a worst-case scenario, investors could withdraw all of their contract value, the GMIB value would decline to zero, and they would be left with nothing to annuitize and, consequently, no future income stream."

Hmmm… We should all be happy that the SEC caught the problem and that MassMutual corrected it (after a hand-slapping and a $1.625 million fine). However, the fact that this product was created and that insurance salesmen were unaware of the terms and consequences of the cap (and thus misleading customers) is troubling, to say the least. And it is a reminder that, when "safe" products have complicated terms and conditions, you have to read the fine print. And you can't just trust the salesman who sold the product to you to explain it to you right. It is the contract itself that will be enforced, not the explanation.

Below are 10 tips to help you navigate a few bank, brokerage and insurance products…

1. **The Fed's Stress Test.**
2. **The 2008 Bailout of AIG.**
3. **Does AIG Own Your Annuity?**
4. **Are Banks Healthy Now?**
5. **Online Discount Brokerages are Healthier Than Legacy Brokerages.**
6. **Not All Bank Products are FDIC-Insured.**
7. **Annuities are Not As Safe As You Think.**
8. **Community Banks Were Hit Hard in the Great Recession.**
9. **Max Out Your 401K First – Before Buying Annuities.**
10. **401k Roll-Overs.**

And here is additional information on these 10 Tips...

1. **The Fed's Stress Test.** On March 13, 2012, the Federal Reserve Board of governors announced the results of their most recent stress test. The media quickly jumped to say that the four lowest-scoring banks, Ally Financial, Citibank, MetLife and SunTrust, "failed." The banks themselves assured their customers and investors that they didn't "fail" the tests, but were simply in need of revising their capital plan, and limiting or eliminating their dividends and buybacks for now. The California state insurance commissioner Dave Jones issued a press release stating that MetLife "exceeds the insurance financial solvency requirements." When I examined the debt of the banks, Citi did not have the highest *reported* debt to equity ratio of the banks. So, while these stress tests are very important, particularly to the continued oversight of these "too big to fail" companies, I wouldn't get overly confident that a bank that *passes* is in great shape.

2. **The 2008 Bailout of AIG.** I'm rather perplexed that a company that needed a $182.3 billion bailout would still be in the financial planning business, in charge of the future of many Americans. However, AIG was and is one of the top mutual fund and annuity providers in

the United States. AIG is still involved in legal matters, hangover from the meltdown, that could be extremely costly. According to the AIG website (on 11.18.12), more than 18 million Americans own an AIG retirement product and the company has over 88 million clients worldwide.

3. **Does AIG Own Your Mutual Fund or Annuity?** Do you own American General mutual funds, life insurance or annuities? Is your retirement plan held by Valic? Western National, SunAmerica, Chartis, SagePoint, Royal Alliance or FSC? These are also AIG companies. If you own a retirement product from one of these companies, you are banking your future on AIG.

4. **Are Banks Healthy Now?** Though 15 major U.S. banks passed the "stress tests," all owe more than they are worth, and most had less revenue in 2011 than the year prior. Banks, like other corporations, can report a quarterly or even annual profit, even when they owe a trillion in debt. Also, the real estate nightmare isn't over. There have been over 12 million homes in the foreclosure process since 2008, with more in the pipeline in the years to come. In some states, like New Jersey, New York, Illinois, Florida and California, it takes years for a bank to foreclose on a property. The banks are also aware that while the homeowner remains

in the home, they water the plants and keep it looking nice. Too many foreclosures in a neighborhood would make real estate prices fall too far too fast, whereas a steady stream of foreclosures is helping to keep the prices more buoyant than they would otherwise be. And these mortgage products are still being swapped around. In other words, U.S. banks are definitely not completely out of the woods yet.

5. **Online Discount Brokerages are Healthier Than Legacy Brokerages.** While the big, bailed out banks owe more than they are worth (sometimes a lot more), TD AMERITRADE and Schwab owe debt that is less than a third of their value. Other legacy brokerages – like Merrill Lynch and Bear Stearns – were bailed out, too. TD AMERITRADE and Schwab, two online discount brokerages, were not a part of the financial meltdown. They both offer FDIC insurance on their investor money market and savings accounts and have the lowest trading fees in the business. Both have banks.

6. **Not All Bank Products are FDIC-Insured.** Insurance company products that a bank sells, including life insurance and annuities, are not covered by the FDIC. More and more, banks and insurance companies are creating products with complicated clauses and scenarios that even the salesmen have a hard time

understanding fully. When purchasing any product from a bank, insurance company or brokerage, you must read the fine print to determine what safety nets are provided. Learn more in FINRA.org's page on Bank Products.

7. **Annuities are Not As Safe As You Think.** If AIG had declared bankruptcy, tens of millions of AIG annuity holders would have been forced to turn to their state guaranty funds in hopes of recovering some of their retirement money. Those funds simply could not have handled the demand. So, it is very important to purchase your insurance and annuity products from companies that are well-managed and financially stable because these products are not FDIC-insured. Learn more about how insurance products are protected by visiting the National Organization of Life and Health Insurance Guaranty Associations (NOLHGA) at www.nolhga.com or the National Conference of Insurance Guaranty Funds (NCIGF) at www.ncigf.org. Since the safety nets are a state function, it's important to know the fiscal health of your state as well.

8. **Community Banks Were Hit Hard in the Great Recession.** 464 banks failed between 2008 and 2012. Most were community banks. The trend slowed in 2012, and consumers with FDIC-protected deposits

were unaffected by the failures. You probably did notice a new sign on the door, however.

9. **Max Out Your 401K First – Before Buying Annuities.** FINRA.org recommends that "most investors should consider an Equity-Indexed Annuity and other annuity products *only* *after* they make the maximum contribution to their 401(k) and other before-tax retirement plans." Why? Because 401Ks are pre-tax investments that reduce your taxable income and allow you to defer taxes on your contribution and investment gains. Learn more in FINRA.org's Investor Alert on Equity-Indexed Annuities.

10. **401k Rollovers.** There are qualifying events where you can rollover your 401K into an online discount brokerage IRA, without penalty. (Check with your CPA for tax guidance on this and with your employer for qualifying event information.) Options include: 1) When you leave your job, 2) When you turn 59 1/2, 3) Certain employer contributions, 4) Post tax contributions, and 5) When the employer changes 401K providers. Rolling over can be a key piece of your profitability plan, especially if your investment options are limited in the 401k, if your employer is paying you in company stock and/or if you just want greater control over where your money is invested. You have

the universe of stocks and funds available to you at the online discount brokers, whereas the 401K provider may only offer you a handful of fund choices. Also, in cases where your employer pays you in company stock, you may be overly reliant on the company's performance, instead of being properly diversified. A general guideline is to have no more than 10% of your nest egg in your own company's stock. Employees at Enron lost far more than they should have, simply by holding too much Enron stock in their 401Ks.

Bottom Line

Bailed out banks and insurance companies are still not healthy, even if they are passing "stress tests." While you may have FDIC insurance to cover your insured bank accounts, the bigger issue is one of trust. Have you read the pages and pages of fine print on the bank products you own? Are you sure that there isn't something in the fine print that could potentially harm you going forward – when you need the money most and least expect it? Have you done a search on the consumer watchdog sites to learn about the experiences of other consumers? You may be a customer of a company that you don't necessarily trust without even knowing it – because you have purchased a product from one of the company's subsidiaries. With regard to annuities, in addition to the risk that you are relying on the health and ethics of one company and that this money is not FDIC-insured, there is a risk that the money you actually receive is less than you are counting on — particularly if that scenario is spelled out in the fine print.

Take-Away Suggestions

1. There are banks and insurance companies that are healthier than others. Do a Stock Report Card to determine which companies you would most like to be a client of.

2. You must read the fine print – all of it – on your life insurance, annuity, CDs and any other new product offered by your bank, brokerage or insurance company.

3. If you are dissatisfied with the options in your 401K, check to see if you can roll it over into a brokerage that offers all of the publicly traded stocks and funds for you. Check for qualifying events that might apply to you at IRS.gov. Enlist the help from the brokerage where you want your funds to be housed. *And* ask the human resources person where you work if any of the qualifying rollover events apply. Remember: don't cash it out! You will experience too many taxes and penalties if you do. Roll it over.

Part 6: Hard Assets

Chapter 18: How to Save Money on Your Electric Bill. Forever.

A few months ago, I wanted to do the math on solar panels. Prices had dropped dramatically, and Michael Liebreich, the CEO of Bloomberg New Energy Finance, was espousing that putting solar panels on your roof was the best investment today. Here is his rationale:

1. Prices on solar panels are a fraction of the price they were just two years ago

2. You're getting almost nothing on your savings

3. It's cheaper to buy the panels than it is to buy energy from your utility. The payback time, with the federal and state subsidies, is down to 4-7 years and the panels last for life (50 years).

4. You are not taxed on any of the savings you get on your electric bill (which is money in your pocket that you're not spending)

5. No money manager can lose your solar panel for you.

For more Michael Liebreich wisdom, check out my interview with him from the August and September 2012 ezines (volume 9, issues 8 and 9).

Solar Panels Offer Returns For Life

So, number one on the list of getting a great return on investment (for life) by investing in a hard asset is this. If you live in a sunny area, consider purchasing solar panels as an investment that not only adds to the value of your home, but also reduces your expenses at a time when you need it most – in retirement, when you don't have any active income, and are relying solely on your investments and Social Security. FYI: Solar panels can be used to provide shade, too; there is no rule that they have to be stacked on the roof. Another benefit to this investment is that savings on your electric bill begin immediately, offering you an instant return on investment. Energy costs are not going to get any cheaper, and it's hard to imagine the incentives getting any better. For most people it will be more cost effective and convenient to connect to the grid, rather than purchasing your own battery backups.

Saving Energy and Money is Much Easier Than You Think

Whether you purchase solar panels or not, reducing your energy usage is another way to enjoy dramatically lower electric bills. Two of the people I interviewed for this article are paying 1/10 of the average costs their neighbors pay – $30/month – simply by modifying their behavior and doing energy efficiency upgrades. If you're paying $30 instead of $300 a month on your electric bill, you're saving $3,240 a year! That saving adds up and compounds, if you're putting the money in a tax-protected retirement account and achieving gains.

Any effort to reduce electrical energy usage requires understanding how energy is measured and billed. Below is a brief description of electrical energy measurement and how it relates to everyday use.

The KWH

Electrical energy consumption is measured in KWH. KWH is defined as kilowatt-hours, or said another way, 1000 watts consumed for an hour. This term is easily adjusted to different rates of consumption, as 2000 watts consumed for half an hour is the same as 1000 watts consumed for one hour, and the same as 500 watts consumed for two hours, or having a 100-watt light bulb on all day (10 hours).

Although this seems easy to understand, keep in mind that the actual rate of energy consumption in your home varies widely as you turn on or off electrical equipment in your house. Some things, like air conditioning and water heaters, use a lot more energy than others. The meter is designed to measure rate of use and time accurately and to add up this consumption for display and billing.

Practical values to consider when identifying energy usage in your home include:

- Wattage of devices you use
- Amount of time they are in use

Keep in mind that for a typical billing cycle of 30 days you have approximately 720 hours, so even those items that use little power add to your bill if allowed to operate 24-7. (One light bulb left on all the time would be 72 KW alone.)

Are Hot Water Heaters and Air Conditioners Needed When You Are At Work?

Some typical household items operate automatically to provide the function they are designed for, such as refrigerators, hot water heaters, air conditioners, etc. Where it is feasible, adjust the set points of these items so that they operate only to the value really needed. The difference in operating time for items such as air conditioners and hot water heaters is greatly influenced by the temperature they are set to maintain. Since items like this use a lot of energy, shortening the amount of time they operate can make a significant difference in your power bill. Turning them off when not needed, for example installing a timer switch on the hot water heater so that it only operates for a few hours in the morning and evening, and adjusting your thermostat up so that your heating or cooling doesn't kick in when no one is home, have the highest potential for energy reduction in a typical home.

Solar Water Heaters

Solar water heaters are a great way to save money on your water heater as well. They are powered by the sun – which is free! There have been dramatic price savings on all clean energy products in the past two years, so, even if you shopped for solar water heaters a few years ago, it's a good idea to check out the prices today. Learn more about solar water heaters at Energy.gov.

Appliances

Other items that use a large amount of energy are electric clothes dryers, ovens, stoves, and heaters. Anything you do to minimize the amount of time such items are in use will reduce your energy consumption. Can you dry two smaller loads of wash at the same time? Of course, not cooking will increase your food bill, and going naked to save on washing and drying will scare the neighbors, so balance this within reason...

Unplug Your Computer and Cell Phone Charger, Turn Off the TV

Look around for items that stay on all of the time, like computers, televisions and cell phone chargers. Most television equipment has an instant-on feature, which requires that they use a reduced amount of power waiting for you to activate them. This is also true of all remote controlled equipment. Even at the sleep-mode, reduced power level may be 10 to 15 watts, which adds up (15 * 720/1000 = 10.8 KWH). Computer equipment, routers, and other such equipment use more power than you might initially think. For example; the laptop I'm using for this article consumes approximately 65 watts. If I leave it plugged in all the time, so that the battery stays topped off for my next remote use, that can cost me 47 KWH on my power bill. Cell phone chargers that are plugged in all the time are energy vampires as well. Power strips with an off/on switch make powering down convenient and easy.

Don't Light Up Empty Rooms

Lights are big users of power, but the most significant thing about them is how long they stay on. Standard incandescent lamps are easy to calculate; a 100-Watt bulb consumes power at a rate of 100 Watts, a 60-Watt bulb consumes power at a rate of 60 Watts. Compact florescent bulbs consume lower amounts of power for approximately the same quantity of light, and their use can be estimated by the wattage indicated on them as well, typical values are 7 to 13 Watts. LED lights have wattage at or below CFLs, with a much longer life than both incandescent and CFLs (with no mercury).

Since the amount of energy you use for lighting is directly proportional to the amount of time you have them tuned on, a good rule of thumb is, "On when you enter; off when you leave."

Energy Efficiency Upgrades

Behavior can go a long way, but it can't solve a drafty room or having your office in shadows, while the empty living room gets all of the natural sunlight. Insulating your home and rethinking the layout from a usage standpoint can also add up to a lot of savings.

I toured a home last month in upstate New York that is one of the most insulated in the United States. The Hudson Passive

Project, designed by Dennis Wedlick and built by Bill Stratton Building Company, according to the Passive House Institute U.S. standards, achieved an amazing feat. In a part of the world that has a very harsh winter, the heat only came on twice! Go to the website PassiveHouse.US to learn more about energy efficiency retrofits, using this impressive, science-based system. In 2012, energy efficiency upgrades were tax-deductible, offering another incentive. Check with your accountant and IRS.gov to learn the rules. This is the kind of home improvement that pays off immediately, *and* when/if you go to sell your home.

Bottom Line Savings

To summarize, electrical energy consumption is billed by rate of use AND amount of time in use, so those who wish to reduce their costs for electrical power have to consider not only how much energy a particular item uses, but how much time it is using that energy.

Controlling energy use requires adjusting one's habits:

1. Turn off lights when unneeded
2. Power down chargers, TVs and computers
3. Should you do some work in the sunny living room in the mornings where there is natural lighting?

Investing in upgrades:

1. Are solar panels and a solar water heater right for you?
2. Do you need to insulate better?
3. Is it time to buy a timer for the water heater or a new energy-efficient refrigerator?

And accepting some lesser degree of comfort to make substantial reductions.

1. Do I need the hot water to be 190 degrees before I mix it with cold water to bathe?
2. Can I adjust to having my house at 75 or 78 degrees instead of 70 (particularly when I'm not there)?
3. Does the refrigerator have to be so cold?

If you learn to analyze the energy consumption of the devices you use each day, you can make conscious decisions on the value you place on using them, as you accept the *real costs* of using them.

This chapter was put together (obviously) using the wisdom of a very experienced, respected electrical engineer. Thanks!

Bottom Line

If you plan on being in your home forever, why not make it an insulated, solar-powered home that costs you almost nothing on your energy bill? This kind of upgrade to your primary residence (and rental property) adds to the top-line value (when/if you sell) and beautifies the bottom line in savings, beginning immediately and continuing for decades to come, as well.

Take-Away Suggestions

1. If you live in a sunny state, check into installing solar panels and connecting to the grid. Consider reaching out to Dan Fink at Buckville.com for additional guidance. Dan is an experienced solar energy contractor who has been living off the grid since 1991.

2. If you are spending obscene amounts of money on your energy bill, it might be time to insulate your home and do other energy efficiency retrofits.

3. Having a very low energy bill, from the investments you make today, could offer one of the best, most reliable return on investment available.

Chapter 19: Gold Investors Beware.

Every year, there is an investment du jour. Everyone tells you that you're crazy if you don't get in *now*. The ads on TV are endless – espousing that this particular investment is the only thing that will be worth anything in the years to come. It was real estate in 2005. It was Dot Com stocks in 2000. And it is gold today.

Many real estate and Dot Com investors were a day late and a dollar short. People who financed their investments, by pulling out home equity or getting a loan, may have lost everything they own. There are already investors today who dumped everything they own into gold, only to be dismayed at how much they have already lost. Even if gold does increase in value in the coming years, and it could, there are many, many ways an investor can be taken advantage of and lose money.

Gold Investors Burned by Goldline

On February 22, 2012, Goldline (the company touted endlessly by Glenn Beck on his former Fox News program) settled with the City of Santa Monica, California (where the company is based) and agreed to pay $5.3 million in restitution to clients. Goldline was forced to stop using deceptive sales tactics, to provide more information and disclosures to clients and to submit to ongoing monitoring at its own expense. In exchange, the City of Santa Monica dismissed criminal charges against the company.

What happened? The City of Santa Monica received numerous complaints from customers who felt that Goldline "scared" them into purchasing gold coins that were worth far less than the purchase price. Instead of having a "safe haven" for their retirement funds, they instantly lost a large portion of their savings. Santa Monica City Attorney Adam Radinsky explained the situation to me, saying, "According to Goldline's own disclosures, the typical markup on the semi-numismatic coin was such that the coin would have to go up 55% for the customer to break even."

What is a semi-numismatic coin? Numismatic coins are supposed to be collectible. So, a semi-collectible coin would be... pretty much just a circular piece of gold bouillon that has been marked up to line the pockets of the company that sells them.

MF Global

MF Global Gold Fund investors were assured they had physical gold. However, those who possessed "warehouse receipts" for their gold holdings were still waiting for the MF Global trustee to approve their claims and release their money as of August 1, 2012 (10 months after the bankruptcy filing). The trustee was having trouble locating all of the missing money. He has to hold some of the assets in reserve until the many lawsuits are resolved. In short, getting your money back is sure to be a lengthy, uphill battle.

What this means for investors, at minimum, is that it is very important to diversify. Don't throw all of your eggs in one gold basket. It's also a reminder that you always want to know the fiscal health of the fund company you are dealing with. For instance, don't just hand over money to any fund or company before finding out how long the company has been in business, how much debt they owe, etc. MF Global was a real company that made some very bad investments in European bonds. However, there are a lot of scam sites out there that can look very legitimate.

Futures

Another way that investors get burned is by buying into gold fever – something that happened to futures investors in late 2011 and 2012. After hitting an all-time high of $1,895/ounce (set on September 5, 2011), gold retreated and was still underwater in November of 2012 – down 8.5%. Investors hoping for gold to top $2000/ounce or higher (we've heard predictions as high as $5,000/ounce) were burned all throughout 2012 – costing options and futures investors a lot of dough.

The Future of Gold

So, is this a temporary stall-out in an otherwise stellar asset? Or will gold return to its place as the worst performing asset over the last 30 years? Gold returned 18% annualized on average for the past ten years, but saw gains of just 4.64%/year over the 30-year period.

There are no guarantees in life, and far fewer in investing, however, whenever an asset performs at three or more times its historical average, it's typically a bubble brewing.

And when the bubble bursts, it's typically quick and long-lived. Investors who bought gold at the $850/ounce high in 1980 had to wait a quarter of a century (29 years) for the value of their gold to return. Most of that time, gold traded between $250-$400/ounce.

Top Holders of Gold

How does the price of gold drop so fast? All it takes is for one or two countries to move in and liquidate a big holding at the highest price. (As you know, when there are more sellers than buyers, the price drops.) Of particular concern today is that Exchange Traded Fund gold investors are in the top five biggest holders of gold in the world. ETF investors can liquidate positions in a matter of seconds – meaning that any move made by a country could be blasted into a hyperspace death spiral by high-frequency traders seeking to sell quickly before the price drops. In this scenario, if gold is a bubble, the prick that bursts the bubble could be a gang, and the deflation could be even more rapid than in times past.

Top Holders of Gold (as of November 2012)

	Country	Gold (in tones)
1.	United States	8,133.5
2.	Germany	3,395.5
3.	IMF	2,814.0
4.	All ETFs	2,500.0
5.	Italy	2,451.8
6.	France	2,435.4
7.	State Street Global Advisors SPDR Gold Shares (symbol: GLD)	1,342.63
8.	China	1,054.1
9.	Switzerland	1,040.1
10.	Russia	934.5
11.	Japan	765.2
12.	Netherlands	612.5
13.	India	557.7
14.	ECB	502.1
15.	Taiwan	423.6
16.	Portugal	382.5
17.	Venezuela	362.0
18.	Saudi Arabia	322.9
19.	United Kingdom	310.3
20.	Turkey	302.4

Source: World Gold Council at Gold.org

Over the last three years, most of the Top 20 countries haven't changed their gold holdings, however ETF investors are still on fire. According to the World Gold Council, in the third quarter of 2012, gold ETF investments increased 56% over the same quarter in 2011. Germany sold a little, while Russia, Taiwan and Turkey increased their holdings. Gold investors pulled back on their interest in gold coins and bars and have focused on funds.

Jewelry Market's Gold Appetite is Down

Walk into an engagement ring store and what you'll discover is that all that glitters is not gold! High prices for gold have pushed designers to use other metals, or gold blends, in their engagement rings. You'll see rose gold (copper/gold blend), white gold (nickel or palladium gold blend), titanium, silver and even palladium, far more than gold rings. 24 karat gold is an expensive rarity. Many couples are opting for "vintage" rings – aka Grandma's – rather than mortgaging their parent's home for an engagement ring. The escalated price of gold is pushing down the demand in the jewelry market. Demand for gold jewelry is down 2% this year over last year.

Crystal Ball: Gold 2013

Gold has had a fantastic run for the last decade, and the party is probably not over yet. This is an emotional play, and in a world of debt, people rightfully want something they can hold onto over "paper" money. (As you see in this section, there are other hard assets that can be very valuable to you.) Personally, I think that if we are entering an Apocalypse, it would be easier to trade a gallon of gas, food or drinking water than gold. No matter what your preference, it is clear that there are a number of ways to get burned on this hot asset, including having someone else hold it for you, like MF Global, or to purchase an "almost collectible coin," from a company like Goldline.

If you're still stuck on gold, another option might be owning a gold mining stock. Know that most of the gold mining companies also have copper and other materials, so they are not a pure play on gold. During tough times, demand for building metals (like copper) tends to level off. Most of the big mining companies had lower revenue in 2012 than 2011.

As I showed you in the Stocks section of this book, it's a better idea to have a hot industry be a slice of your pie, rather than to go all in. And you definitely need to evaluate your hot funds at least once a year, and capture your profits.

Below is an illustration of exactly why that is the case.

The Gold Crash of 1980. A Brief History of Gold.

Gold hit $850/ounce one day in 1980, and then dropped a hundred bucks the next. Learn how not to buy into fool's gold, and why this great gilded asset is riskier than you think.

On January 21, 1980, gold hit an all-time high price (for that period) of $850/ounce.

Then, quite unexpectedly and overnight, the price fell by more than $100, to $737.50/ounce, and continued to drop throughout the rest of the year. By the end of 1980, gold had fallen 31% from it's high, to $589.75/ounce.

The following year, in 1981, gold prices fell another $200/ounce for an average price of $410/ounce (less than ½ of $850), and then plunged again, to a low of $300/ounce in 1982. Imagine how desperate the gold rush buyers at the top felt within two short years!

Gold Prices 1980-1984 and 2002-2008

Year	Beginning Price	Ending Price	High Price
1980	$559.50	$589.75	$850.00
1981	$597.50	$397.50	$599.25
1982	$395.00	$456.90	$481.00
1983	$449.50	$382.40	$509.25
1984	$383.00	$309.00	$405.85
2002	$278.35	$347.20	$327.05
2005	$427.75	$513.00	$535.50
2006	$530.00	$632.00	$725.00
2007	$639.75	$833.75	$841.10
2008	$846.75	$869.75	$971.50

Source: Kitco.com

As you can see from the above chart, gold prices ping-ponged around in the $300-$400/ounce range for over two decades. The person who purchased gold for $850/ounce in 1980 had to wait until 2008 to get their money back in full – 29 years.

Boom! Crash! Gold in 1980 fell just as far, faster, than real estate in 2006 and Dot Com in 2000. In fact, it is very likely that the same folks who encouraged you to buy more house than you could afford in 2006, or to hold your cash negative AOL in 2000 (due to the New Economy) are now the authors of the new fairytale – that gold will become the only currency in a bankrupt Western World.

With all of the gold ads on TV these days, what you might not be aware of is that even though gold has been on a tear for the last decade, scoring 18% annualized gains, on average, gold was killed again by stocks in 2009. NASDAQ scored gains of 40% in 2009, while gold prices rose only 26%. That trend repeated in 2012, when NASDAQ scored gains of up to 18% on the year, while gold was down by 8-10% over that same period. Small, mid cap and even large cap growth stocks were stronger than gold during 2009, in the wake of the Great Recession. Only the Dow Jones Industrial Average (which has a hefty composition of bailouts and legacy value stocks) performed worse.

Performance of Stocks and Gold in 2009

Asset	Gains in 2009
NASDAQ	40%
US mid-cap stocks	38%
US large-cap growth	36%
US small-cap growth	35%
Gold price	26%
Dow Jones Industrial Average	15%

Bottom Line

Is gold for fools or 24 karat in 2013 and beyond? Gold, like all commodities, is primarily controlled by simple laws of supply and demand. A rally can be killed overnight if a big seller dumps a hefty load. Prices spike when central governments buy gold en masse to issue coins to hungry buyers or when ETF brokerages make it easy as a click to buy a gold index, as is the case in today's marketplace.

Take-Away Suggestions

1. Remember that gold is an emotional purchase, and that even when it is hot, hot, hot, it's a better idea to have just a piece of your investment strategy dependent upon this volatile asset.

2. Savvy (or unscrupulous) gold brokers and sellers feed investor froth with talks of the Apocalypse, anticipating that many people, especially in times of high unemployment, low consumer confidence and/or inflation, will throng to buy high.

3. Just as reliably, when hoarding gold becomes the investment du jour and prices reach astronomical heights, big players move in en masse to take their profits and dump their holdings. Prices can fall dramatically in a very short period of time.

Chapter 20: Real Estate, Income Property and Consumer Staples Businesses

If you have a lot of money "safe" in paper assets, it's a good idea to consider turning your paper into something real – before inflation hits, particularly since you are not likely to ever see such low financing rates in your lifetime. The same is true for younger investors who are interested in escaping the rat race.

There are many ways to buy into hard assets, particularly if you open up your creative thinking. Explore the available options with an accountant, so that you understand all of the ways that you might leverage your pension, annuity, 401K, IRA, etc., with the minimal amount of penalties and taxes, before you dismiss this as out of reach for you. If you have a small net worth, but a good income or great credit, keep reading as well. Some of the ideas below might spark how you can use your assets, in combination with complimentary assets of a partner, to invest in income-producing investments that also have the potential for being worth more in the years to come.

Wonder if investing in real estate or a consumer staples business is right for you? Use my 3-Ingredient Recipe for Cooking Up Profits as your guide.

Three-Ingredient Investment Recipe for Cooking Up Profits

1. Start with what you know and love.
2. Pick the leader in the sector (in real estate, it's location, location, location).
3. Buy low; sell high (easy to say; hard to do).

Take the steps in order. There is no reason to consider price if you aren't sure that you have a winning investment. (Gold at any price in the 25-year period between 1980 and 2002 was a loser, as was real estate in 2005 and Dot Com in 2000.) And you can't really pick a leader in anything before you have educated yourself on at least the fundamentals. (Getting the low down from a salesman who will get paid a commission if they sell you something is not the same as really getting to know the investment opportunity that you are interested in).

Having said that, I have to admit. I, like you, am interested in real estate and hard assets because real estate prices are, on average, at a 10-year low, while interest rates are lower than they've ever been. Ever. That is a window I never expect to see again in my lifetime, and I'm not going to let it pass me by.

But, in order to be successful, I must still use my template.

1. Start with what you know and love.

Franchise Opportunities: Whether you are interested in a Chipotle franchise, a car wash, student housing or adult day-care, each one of these investments is going to have upsides and downsides. The upside for Chipotle is that demand is high for healthy, fast food. The downside is that you might get stuck in the server line if one of your employees is late for work. That makes this active income, not passive – something that is not an option for you, if you are a professional with a demanding job.

So, how do you start knowing more about a food franchise? Start by working at one, at least for a week. Interview owners. Seek out the wisdom of executives at Score.org. Score offers experienced mentors for free to small business owners.

Real Estate: Real estate prices are at a 10-year low in many markets, and it is cheaper to buy than it is to rent in many cities. However, rentals can have more costs than you might be aware of. Does the city have strong rent control laws? Also, there is a glut of supply in a lot of cities, meaning that you might have to come up with a competitive edge to attract quality renters. The more you know about the kind of neighborhood you want to own in and the type of renter you wish to attract, the more likely you will make a cash-positive, winning investment.

Collectibles: Some people, like Jay Leno, would rather own classic cars than income property. However, buying low and selling high in classic cars, or artwork, or jewelry, requires factoring in insurance and storage costs. You also have to know the product well enough to make sure you are not getting a fake, or buying into something that will fall apart, or overpaying. Finally, make sure that the appetite of the marketplace will remain hungry going forward. Will stamps lose value in a world where everyone emails, or will they become even more treasured? While you might think this is a guess, you can analyze real data and see where things stand today to inform where the future is headed.

2. Pick the leader in the sector (in real estate, it's location, location, location).

If you've determined that you want to own income property, now you have the task of picking the best possible building and neighborhood. If you purchase in a neighborhood with bars on the windows, you're not going to be able to rent to a young, upwardly mobile professional or couple. Pick a place where you will have some pride of ownership.

When thinking of the business to own, pick a business that will do well in tough times and is also part of some emerging trend. Mystery meat has made health-conscious consumers more interested in sustainably produced meats and produce. Is now the right time to buy an old-school fast food joint?

Would you rather own a smoothie counter inside a popular workout facility or try to compete with that counter by purchasing a store two doors down?

Taking the time to really pick the leader in the sector has a better chance of paying off now and going forward than just jumping in blind.

Kick the dirt yourself. Look at the neighborhood in the morning and at night. Know the kind of customer you want to attract, and make sure that you are picking a location where that customer is likely to come. If you are planning on renting, make sure the neighborhood isn't glutted with vacancies, and see what renters are paying for other places that are similar to yours. (Don't just rely upon the comps, make a few calls and read a few signs and ads yourself.)

Buy low; sell high (easy to say; hard to do).

Do the math yourself. Do not rely upon the agent to get the comps right.

I recently looked at a deal in a premium neighborhood that held very little interest for me – because all of the assumptions were on the high end, meaning that the only way investors make money is if a dream-come-true scenario played out. It also happened to be on an unproven corner with low customer traffic, whereas all of the assumptions were based upon the traffic in the very popular neighborhood, with 100 times the traffic, one street away.

Below are more tips to help you determine if you are picking the leader and making a sound investment.

Consider Your Costs to Carry the Investment

Let's take a multi-use building in a great neighborhood as an example.

1. **Vacancy**. Is the deal based upon 5% vacancy? This is clearly a best-case scenario. Is there any scenario where vacancy could be much higher? It would be twice as high at just 10% vacancy. (Answering this question requires you to return to Ingredient #1 – know your investment well.) If you doing a remodel, the place will be vacant during the renovation. That increases the vacancy rate, at least for the remodel period. Also, each time you acquire a new tenant, there is downtime to fix up the rental. Is this an area with a lot of students that leave at the end of the term?

2. **Maintenance.** With rental property, there are regular wear and tear, irregular wear and tear, and turnover maintenance costs. Regular wear and tear can include plumbing, roofing and landscaping. You can expect something to wear out at least once every seven or eight years. Unexpected maintenance costs include someone stuffing the toilet with baby wipes, flooding, earthquakes, fires and other natural disasters. (There is a deductible on the insurance, plus there are always things that the insurance doesn't cover or short-changes you on.) Every time your tenant leaves, you have to paint, at minimum, and perhaps replace the carpeting and a few appliances.

3. **Insurance.** While this line item is obvious, the potential for an unpleasant surprise is not. In some areas of the nation, insurance costs have skyrocketed in the past few years. On the East Coast, flood insurance is so high it is almost unaffordable for many homeowners, without breaking their budget or draining their nest egg. Do not rely on the comps for this price. Get your own estimate. It might have changed since the comp was written up.

4. **Taxes.** Taxes fluctuate wildly across the states. Since most states are in the same kind of trouble that the U.S. is, make sure that you test the winds of the current political climate. Are property taxes likely to increase in the near future? Is this one of the states that is really in

the hole? Could there be a push to raise revenue at the homeowner's expense?

5. **Capital Financing**. The most obvious solution is to go to a bank. However, if your credit makes this out of reach, can you put together a group of investors? Can you approach a friend or family member for the financing? If you are a friend or family member, you have to do your due diligence and make sure that the business and/or property doesn't have other lien holders attached. Do not loan money to a desperate homeowner who is trying to hang onto a home they cannot afford. That is just giving money to the bank and may not help the homeowner in the least – beyond buying them one or two months. It would be a much better idea to purchase a new home, at today's prices, and offer a lease option to your friend – if you are sure they would make a good renter. (You are shooting yourself in the foot if you rent to someone without a job. That requires charity, not an investment, and comes from a different part of your budget – within reason.)

6. **Income**. When calculating the income be sure to include all of the variables. It's better to be conservative than optimistic in terms of income. It would have to be a competitive rent, in a popular neighborhood, with a resilient economy, in a pristine building, to justify 5%

vacancy rates. If you are planning a remodel, factor in that loss of income. (No one will be renting while the place is torn apart.)

7. **Remodels and Upgrades.** Be conservative about the time it will take to get the job done. Unfortunately, due to stringent codes and the unreliability of subcontractors, I typically add a lot of time and money to the estimate. My foolproof remodel ratio is to times the budget by three and the time by 10. If the contractor said he'd get it done in one month, I allowed ten months. If the cost was going to be $10,000, I passed up the offer if I didn't think I could afford $30,000. You might think that sounds insanely conservative, but unfortunately, it was spot on twice. I always came in on time and on budget, using this formula. You have no idea just how much extra time one code violation, or one subcontractor not showing up on time, can cost you until you've done a construction project.

8. **Equity.** The great news about purchasing at a 10-year low (in many markets throughout the U.S.) is that your potential for upside is better than it has been in a decade. Unfortunately, that is not a guarantee that the value of your property will increase immediately and robustly. There is simply too much inventory in many markets for you to buy and flip for a profit. Shadow inventory held by the banks and properties that have

been in the pipeline, awaiting foreclosure, for years are much higher than you know, particularly in the judicial foreclosure states. So, your equity plan should include a strategy that makes sense for a longer period of time – 5-7 years, at minimum.

Turning Paper Assets Into Real Estate

401Ks, IRAs, etc.: You don't want to take a big penalty or pay a lot of taxes, so cashing out your 401K, for anyone under 59 1/2, is not the best idea. If you are under 60, can you borrow against it? Can you use your nest egg to secure the capital or to get a lower interest rate? In the case where you are using your nest egg as leverage, be sure that you get the nest egg money that you are leveraging as safe as possible, so that you are not subject to market fluctuations. You still need safe, liquid assets, too.

Pensions: Some legacy corporations, including Ford, are offering buyouts on their pensions. Should you take the buyout and invest in income property? Only you know the right answer to this. When making your determination, take a look at what happened to others, when their company went through restructuring. If you work for an auto manufacturer, take a look at the pensions of GM and Chrysler. If you work for an airline, check out what is happening to American Airline's employees. Even if you work for a company like General

Electric or Wal-Mart, do a Stock Report Card on your company, paying particular attention to the earnings growth, debt and profit margins, to determine the likelihood of having your pension reduced down the road.

Annuities: Are you sure that your annuity is going to pay what you believe it will? Have you read the fine print on your policy? Is your distribution subject to the stock or bond market? Is your annuity provider more vulnerable than you know? Do a Stock Report Card on your annuity provider, paying particular attention to the earnings growth, debt and profit margins, to determine the likelihood of having any problems with your annuity down the road.

Partnering: Some people have a great income, or a big nest egg, but lousy credit. Some people have good credit, but make a lower income and have a smaller nest egg. If you have a piece of the solution, then look for a partner who can complete the picture. Remember that if you purchase income property, the rental income is part of the income considered when you go to finance the transaction.

Even if you had to give a home back, is it possible that your retired parents would be better off buying a home and renting it to you, on a lease option basis, than for them to continue to have their nest egg at risk, with you renting from a stranger? Would they be willing to be your financing, at 7% interest, if their money were secured by your home? Will they co-sign your loan?

If you are loaning the money, you must consider the risk of renting to someone you love – particularly if you are relying on that income to eat. Strike a deal that protects you, and put it in writing.

Free Money: At today's ultra-low interest rates, money is almost free. Of course, it is difficult to access because lending standards are so tight. For most people this means that you have to partner up or form a limited liability company or partnership to access the financing necessary to fund income property.

Small Businesses

Most small businesses are not successful. There is an extremely high belly-up rate and most small business owners work very long hours. That is why I have listed "consumer staples" small businesses, rather than passion businesses. If you are interested in being a franchise owner, or owning some car washes, or drive-through Starbucks, you are benefitting from buying into a business that has already proven itself to be a success. This is very different from launching your own mobile phone app business. Still, even with an established franchise, do not cut corners when you are considering such a serious shift of focus. Do the math. Kick the dirt. Use the recipe. Make sure your company is not at risk of losing market share.

Hard Assets vs. Paper Assets

Let's say you have a $500,000 nest egg and are 60, getting ready to retire in five years. If you lost $200,000 in the Great Recession, you definitely want to make sure that never happens again. If you take $400,000 and purchase income property (making sure to do the proper evaluation before you do), then you now have $400,000 in property (with a good rental income each month and the potential for the property to increase in value), with $100,000 in your nest egg.

When you are diversifying, according to the pie charts in the Stocks section of this book, you redraft your pie chart using only the $100,000 that you have left in your nest egg. (Again, the $400,000 in property is part of your estate, but it is not "liquid," so do not include its value in the Modern Portfolio Theory stock and bond diversification). Be sure to take extra care to get safe, according to the wisdom outlined in the Bonds section of this book. As I've said so many times in this book, safe means not at risk of capital loss (loss of the amount you invest). Don't reach for yield.

Bottom Line

Hard assets will outperform paper assets in the coming years. However, you must do a careful evaluation to determine which hard asset will best match your personality. And if you have good income, but no credit, or good credit, but no down payment, partnering might be your best option.

Take-Away Suggestions

1. Use the 3-Ingredient Recipe for Cooking Up Profits to focus your analysis on any hard asset you might wish to invest in.

2. Evaluate all of your paper assets, including your pension and your annuity, by doing a "stress" test of your own on the company that is underwriting your future (i.e. a Stock Report Card, at minimum). Is that company financially secure enough to bank your future on? Should you "take a hit" – extricate yourself from the bank or insurance product or mutual fund – and use the money to buy into a hard asset that could be more inflation-proof and income producing?

3. There is a big difference between owning a big name franchise and an Internet startup (or any other new business). An unproven new business has a high risk of failing, which puts it out of the "money while you sleep" category. You should not take that kind of risk with your nest egg. (However, you can fund a startup with fun or education money.)

AFTERWORD:
The ABCs of Prosperity and Abundance.

I first went on record that the U.S. was entering "Japan-like stagnation" in 2006, when high oil prices, legacy costs, escalating commodity and materials prices and a real estate bubble had me worried. (I had warned that the real estate bubble was poised to pop in April of 2005 – which turned out to be right at the high.) Here's an excerpt of an article I did on this subject from the March 2006 ezine (volume 3, issue 3).

Corporations with defined benefit plans are underwater on their pension obligations by a whopping $450 billion, while the public sector pensions are drowning by an additional $260 billion (source: Milken Institute). The airline industry has lost approximately $42 billion since 2000 and is carrying over $100 billion in debt, according to Airport Transportation Association VP & chief economist John Heimlich. General Motors lost $8.6 billion in 2005, driven by "poor performance" and legacy costs, *according to GM chairman and CEO Rick Wagoner. Clearly the aging of the U.S. population, alongside escalating medical costs and global competition is wiping out some industries, especially those that provide defined benefit plans to their workers and retirees.*

All of the issues we are dealing with today, as a crisis, were evident in 2006. All of the factors I've outlined in this book as drags on GDP – the high cost of oil, legacy promises, medical costs – are still critically in need of addressing. There is a lot of talk about cutting spending, but each party covets only part of the solution and eschews other important elements. We must become more educated and united about the key issues that will ensure our collective and personal abundance and prosperity — kicking our oil addiction, getting healthy and fit, helping our businesses and corporations deal with legacy promises that they are having difficulty keeping and educating our population for the jobs of tomorrow. Making it easy for people to start a business cannot carry any nation on its own, although it is absolutely the foundation of freedom and democracy.

Just as you have to address the big-ticket items in your own budget in order to live within your means, the U.S. has to address the big-ticket spending to reduce the debt and balance our own budgets. There is "good debt" that pays off for you personally, and there are also certain national budget items that are investments for our collective future. Energy independence (not fossil fuel addiction), healthy citizens, a business friendly environment and a focus on STEAM (Science, Technology, Engineering, the Arts and Math) education are all investments that pay off, and are the foundation of America. (In the nascent oil industry, we were supplying our own, instead of importing from other countries.) Imagine how fast we could get back on track if every American embraced these reforms in their own lives, on their own doorstep and in their own communities! Collectively, we would be saving trillions of dollars and going a long way to reducing our national debt.

If 1/3 of Americans weren't obese, we wouldn't have to spend $2.5 trillion each year on health care. If everyone drove a fuel-efficient car or rode a bike (like they do in Amsterdam), we wouldn't have to spend $420 billion importing oil and petroleum products each year. That could lead to fewer military engagements in the Middle East, another multi-trillion dollar savings. Now that people are living longer, healthier lives, the golden years can be more productive. When we manage our own financial future, we can do a far better job than handing that over to a corporation that might not be able to compete in a few decades.

So, what's the solution to getting the U.S. economy back on track?

1. **Energy Independence**. And by that I mean kick the oil habit, adopt clean energy and make our cities more bike friendly. We cannot remain enslaved and indebted to the fossil fuels industry. As Michael Liebreich, the CEO of Bloomberg New Energy Finance reminds us, "No country can develop with that sort of a drag on its economy." Oil production is up and demand is down in the United States since 2008, however, we have to use imported oil when we are fighting wars in the Middle East. Therefore, producing more oil in the Gulf of Mexico or Canada won't make us energy independent. Additionally, increased demand from China and India is pushing up oil prices – another factor we have no control over. Getting more fuel-efficient personally will go a long way to helping you balance your own budget, too.

2. **Health**. 1/3 of our population is obese. Obesity causes a lot of health issues and is certainly a large contributor to the $2.5 trillion Americans pay on health care every year. Mike Milken, the chairman of the Milken Institute, says, "If everyone in America lost weight and returned to the same weight levels of 1991, we would

save one trillion dollars. We would cover all the uninsured, and we would be able to quadruple the money for medical research." Health is the best health insurance. Focusing on health will help your fiscal health, too.

3. **Financial Literacy.** Getting financially literate and taking charge of our own lives and future – because we'll do a much better job for ourselves than the legacy corporations did for our grandparents – is the key to personal financial freedom. If we make smart choices about our retirement plans, we invest in companies that are run well – rather than having blind faith in companies that would be bankrupt if we had not bailed them out. We vote with our dollars on which companies will succeed and which ones will fold, encouraging those that make the best products and services. When we are financially literate, we go back to having free choice, instead of cronyism economics. We also have a shot at living our own dream life, if we invest well.

4. **STEAM Education.** We must educate Americans for the jobs of tomorrow, with an emphasis on STEAM – science, technology, engineering, the arts and math.

There have been over three million unfilled jobs in the U.S. throughout the Great Recession and continuing. The problem is having qualified individuals to fill those jobs. And yet, it cannot be all left-brain learning. Creativity, risk-taking and entrepreneurialism are at the heart of innovation. And our kids not only enjoy learning more, but actually learn better, through the arts.

5. **Thrive Budgets™**. If each American placed an emphasis on health, on fuel efficiency and on education that would go a long way to cutting spending. The U.S. would import less oil, pay less money on health care and fill those three million unfilled jobs. Yes, due to the high debt, and the amount of time it will take to transition to a healthier, leaner, better educated America across the land, we *all* need to give a little now – which will feel like a lot.

However, while we cut spending, we cannot sacrifice the jobs of tomorrow, the products of tomorrow or the tools that will allow Americans to take on the rich task of managing their own retirements. In other words, well-educated, healthy and confident citizens, who are ready to roll up their sleeves and work, are a huge piece of what makes America great and must continue to be, if we want to erase the debt and lead in a global marketplace.

While Congress is in charge of the budgets for our nation, we are in charge of our lives. And there is a lot that we can do personally, with our family and friends, to promote a healthier nest egg, a happier family and a prosperous nation – to take control of our budgets and debt, and get safe from the boom and bust cycles that are fueled by free, easy money and high-octane traders. It is my mission to continue providing forensic, investigative financial news, information and education, as found in the pages of *The ABCs of Money, You Vs. Wall Street* (aka *Put Your Money Where Your Heart Is)*. I intend to continue publishing the NataliePace.com ezine and hosting my Investor Educational Retreats, to empower you to become the architect of your dream money house. (You can still hire contractors to build it for you, if you wish.)

When you are richer and happier, you are better able to improve yourself, your family and your community. When you are educated and informed, you are more capable of successful investing in passive income projects and co-creating, with your partners, a more beautiful tomorrow. When you rely on debt collectors to design your get out of debt plan, or salesmen to design your investment strategy and your family budget, you'll end up with a design that benefits them – often at your expense. When someone says, "Let me do it for you," prepare to be oppressed. When someone says, "Let me teach you how," prepare to fly.

The ABCs of abundance and prosperity are simple really. At the heart of it is one maxim – Always Be Creating. It's the key to success for business, for individuals and for collective endeavors, such as nations.

If you want to fly, you have to lighten your load. So the process of cutting back on basic needs, in order to thrive more, is actually what frees you up to enjoy life.

Every cent you own and every moment you spend is always an investment. So use your time, talent and money to create something great – great health, educated, empowered children and teens, and a beautiful bottom line.

Yes, you can have it all — when you have a well-designed plan.

Yours in peace and prosperity,
Natalie Wynne Pace

APPENDIX: FREE
SAMPLE PIE CHARTS

Sample 2012 Nest Egg (assuming you are 50)

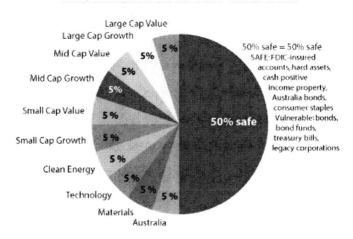

Sample 2012 Nest Egg (assuming you are 25)

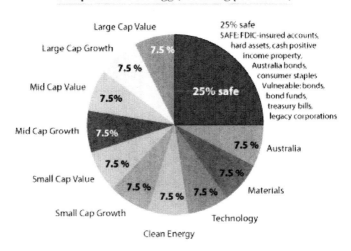

ACKNOWLEDGEMENTS:

First and foremost, I offer thanks to my family – my wild and gifted son, my talented, intelligent and good-looking brother and sisters, my faithful, thoughtful father, my courageous, groundbreaking mother (my inspiration), my smart, beautiful and caring daughter, the many wonderful women who have "mothered" me, my aunts and uncles, and my fun, loyal friends whom I consider to be my family, too. Thank you also to my foster families, who protected me and provided for me while I was still in school. You know who you are, and please know that I am forever grateful.

Thanks so much to the creative, can-do team at Waterfront, led by Bill Gladstone and Jack Jennings, with support from Maureen Maloney and Vanessa Chalmers. Kenneth Kales at Kales Press provided very important support, while Jeffrey Yozwiak at Vook was patient and expeditious throughout the process. It's a lot of fun to cut the publishing time down to a month from a year! This is not possible without a team of this caliber, and I feel very blessed indeed to have worked with them.

To my advisory team, who provide important wisdom and perspective, you know I couldn't do it without you. Thanks to St. JJM, Harriet Mouchley-Weiss, Diane Mkitarian and Andrew Frank.

To my friends in various cities, who always make me feel like visiting royalty, thank you Diane, Matt, Carmel, Kevin, Claire, Brenda, Justine at Tor Royal (Princetown, UK), Victoria at Le Parker Meridien (NYC), The Ritz London, The Ritz-Carlton Hotel (everywhere), Restormel Manor House and Cottages (Cornwall, England), Ballyfin (Ireland), Barnsley House (Cotswolds, England), Calcot Manor Hotel (Cotswolds, England) and Hotel Negresco (Nice, France) – and Maria for helping with the arrangements.

Sunil Rampersad and Sam Bartells have been managing my website and publishing my ezine through thick and thin for over a decade now! Thank you so much. I'm forever indebted to Heather, my right hand, who works so hard to share our content with all of our subscribers.

The team at the Ambrose Hotel in Santa Monica, led by Claudio Henrique, have been hosting my Investor Educational Retreats in style and sustainability for many years.

The contributing writers at NataliePace.com are some of the brightest and best in the entire world. Thank you Dr. Gary Becker, Judge Richard A. Posner, Kay Koplovitz, Ben

Acknowledgements:

Horowitz, Dan Fink, Marilyn Tam, Dr. Marc Miles, Paul Woods and the many other experts, VIPs and policymakers whom I have featured at important moments throughout the challenging last decade, including HRH The Prince of Wales, Her Majesty Queen Noor of Jordan, Joe Moglia, Dr. Lawrence Yun, Michael Liebreich and Ambassador Melanne Verveer.

Finally, thank you to all of the brilliant friends and colleagues who hit the ball of economic debate over the net with me. Thank you for always treating me like a member of the club – even when I was just beginning to establish my track record. Much love always! And please keep the compelling debate, data and statistics forthcoming.

Photo by Marie Commiskey. AvalonPhotography.com.

Natalie Wynne Pace is the author of The ABCs of Money and You Vs. Wall Street (aka Put Your Money Where Your Heart Is). She is the founder and CEO of the Women's Investment Network, LLC (a global financial news, information and education site), with a mission of adding a splash of green to Wall Street and transforming lives on Main Street™. Natalie's books and articles have been saving homes and nest eggs for more than a decade, while at the same time earning her the prestigious ranking of #1 stock picker. Natalie Pace is a blogger on HuffingtonPost.com and a repeat guest on national television and radio shows such as Good Morning America, Fox News, CNBC, ABC-TV, PBS, Forbes.com, NPR and more. As a strong believer in giving back, she has been instrumental in raising tens of millions for public schools, financial literacy, the arts and underserved women and girls worldwide. Follow her on Twitter.com/NataliePace and Facebook.com/NatalieWynnePace. For more information please visit NataliePace.com.

Book Cover Design by Sunil Rampersad.

CPSIA information can be obtained at www.ICGtesting.com
Printed in the USA
LVOW06s1226160415

434865LV00002B/231/P